The Wheel of the Year

The Wheel of the Year

**Your Nurturing Guide
to Discovering Nature's
Seasons and Cycles**

REBECCA BEATTIE

Elliott&Thompson

First published 2022 by
Elliott and Thompson Limited
2 John Street
London WC1N 2ES
www.eandtbooks.com

ISBN: 978-1-78396-679-0

9 8 7 6 5 4 3 2 1

A catalogue record for this book is available from the British Library.

Typesetting: Marie Doherty
Printed by CPI Group (UK) Ltd, Croydon, CR0 4YY

CONTENTS

Introduction vii

ONE Midwinter or Yule 1

TWO Imbolc or Candlemas 29

THREE Spring Equinox 55

FOUR May Eve or Beltane 77

FIVE Midsummer or Summer Solstice 103

SIX Lammas 123

SEVEN Autumn Equinox 141

EIGHT November Eve or Samhain 163

Desideratum, or the Manifesto of Perfectly Imperfect 189

Acknowledgements 193

References 195

Further Reading 199

INTRODUCTION

I wasn't born a witch. Few people of my generation were, although I have encountered the odd one along the way. I am not the seventh daughter of a seventh daughter. I had no moments of envisioning the goddess while driving down the motorway. In fact, I was brought up in a rural community that was largely Anglican, although, looking back, the signs were there. My favourite time of year was harvest festival. We would decorate the church with autumn flowers – red poppies and orange chrysanthemums, interwoven with ears of wheat – and bring food to donate to those who needed it most. In those services, the readings were all focused on nature, and the season of creation. That service made me feel more at home than any other. Despite the long years of involvement in the local routine of the church, I always felt out of place and alienated by the lack of a feminine divine presence. I studied comparative religions at school and was fascinated by other people's traditions, not realising at the time I was seeking something, though it took me a bit longer to realise that I wasn't quite the agnostic I believed I was. At eighteen, I left home and village life behind me and set off in search of adventure and an acting career, which is what I was certain I was born to do.

Funny how life changes the map and leaves us wondering if we somehow missed a turn. Fast forward about a decade: I was in my late twenties and based in London when the penny dropped. I had an active social life, I was involved in a bountiful creative venture running a film collective with my two best friends, I was touring the country performing in *Macbeth*, my favourite of Shakespeare's plays – but I was feeling dissatisfied and out of sorts. I had just broken up from a significant relationship and I was frustrated that I hadn't been earning my income through acting, but it was more than that. I was experiencing a phenomenon that modern witches or pagans refer to as their 'Saturn Returns'. In astrological terms, it means that the planet Saturn – the sphere that governs stability and foundations – has come back into your chart at the position it was in when you were born. In simpler terms, my world as I knew it was ending.

Everything started to look shaky when I put it under the magnifying glass, and I started rethinking all my life decisions. On tour, we were staying in farmhouses, surrounded by nature at every turn. I was getting up with the sunrise, walking in the rural landscape and spending contemplative time in solitude surrounded by trees and fields. I had time to breathe the air and inspiration flowed in. This was what had been lacking in my life. In all the urban streets I walked down to auditions, in all the dusty rehearsal rooms, and the admin jobs I took to pay the rent, I had been missing my connection to nature and, more importantly, I had been looking in the wrong place for fulfilment – I had been seeking outside myself. My journey to self-discovery had begun.

When I returned to London from that tour of *Macbeth*, I knew I had found my spiritual peace in nature and that there must be more to life than the misery of hard-nosed rejections I was experiencing in my acting career. I set off in search of meaning, intending to return to acting once I had found my way back to a more fulfilled and fulfilling life. This path led to my training in Wicca.

Don't be alarmed if you've not heard that term 'Wicca' before, or if it makes you wonder if I am a little peculiar. (I really am – but then, aren't we all?) I will tell you more about it as we go on. For now, all you need to know is that it is a spiritual way of life that centres on our sacred connection to nature.

It was on this path that I learned all about the Wheel of the Year, a concept that helped me to understand my place in the world, to deepen that connection to nature I had felt when touring the countryside and to appreciate fully the wonders of its cycle, no matter the season – or location.

There are various ways of carving up the year into smaller, more manageable time periods. Our Graeco-Roman months of the year are one way, but other faiths also have their own methods of measuring time. For pagans, since the 1940s or 1950s, the year has been defined and delineated by the Wheel of the Year. Yet this seasonal calendar is now spreading outwards and connecting with nature lovers more widely. If you have spent any time on social media over the last few years, you will probably have encountered it. #witchesofinstagram is one of the most followed tags around, WitchTok is a thing, and people have become very curious about modern paganisms, including druidry, heathenism, witchcraft and the many other spiritual faiths that sit beneath the pagan umbrella and follow the Wheel of the Year. However, you certainly don't have to identify as pagan to find meaning in the Wheel: as long as you are a lover of nature and want to spend more time there, reflecting, observing, dreaming, creating, healing, then the Wheel of the Year can help you to do just that.

The Wheel is best thought of as being represented by an old-fashioned wagon wheel (not the biscuit). The year is divided into eight festivals – known as sabbats – that are observed by pagan groups across the world marking a particular moment in the cycle of the natural world with a day of contemplation and celebration. Each sabbat occurs every six weeks or so, and our celebratory practices are always a reflection of what is happening in nature at that time. So following the Wheel enables us to stay connected to the earth as

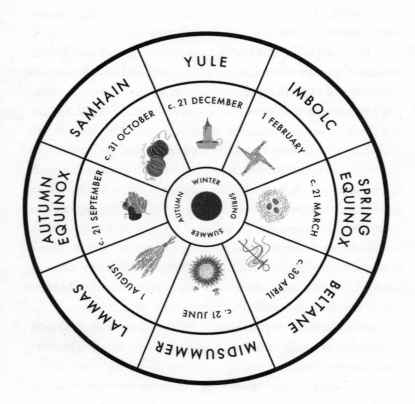

we move through the seasons. The purpose of this book is to help you to do the same, to guide you through each sabbat and find your own connection to nature and yourself.

Some of these eight festivals have their origins in the Celtic cultures of Europe, but the history of the others requires a little more discernment. The Wheel as a cohesive whole is not as ancient as one might believe . . . Well, it is and it isn't. Let me explain.

The Wheel of the Year was brought together by two men – Ross Nichols (the father of Modern Pagan Druidry) and Gerald Gardner (the father of Modern Pagan Witchcraft) in the 1950s and 1960s. They were inspired by theories of an ancient witch cult and the idea of a more shamanic, nature-based, indigenous faith, one that had existed before Christianity came to the British Isles. The trouble was that while archaeological studies have certainly proved that such faiths existed before the arrival of the Romans, they relied largely on an oral tradition and much of the meaning behind the practices had since been lost. Undeterred, Nichols and Gardner began to build new traditions of paganism using nature as their principal inspiration for developing a relationship with the divine. It was a logical consequence that those practices, rooted in the cycles of Mother Earth, would come to form this Wheel of the Year.

Nichols' Druids began celebrating quarter days: the solstices and equinoxes, which mark the beginning of each quarter of the year (traditionally when rents and other payments were due). Meanwhile Gardner's witches were celebrating the Celtic equivalents, which had become known as cross-quarter days as they fell in between the others. In the late 1950s the two practices merged, and the Wheel of the Year was born. Since that time, modern pagans have organised their practices around it, with the following sabbats:

Yule or Midwinter – 21 December
Imbolc – 1 February

Spring equinox – 21 March
Beltane or May Eve – 30 April
Midsummer – 21 June
Lammas – 1 August
Autumn equinox – 21 September
Samhain or November Eve – 31 October

(The exact dates can vary due to Earth taking slightly more than 365 days to travel around the sun, hence the need for leap years.)

I have been teaching people about the pagan Wheel of the Year for several years now at a bookshop in Bloomsbury called Treadwell's. Treadwell's has an important place in the lives of many people, and seekers come from all over the world to visit. In the UK we live in a climate that allows us to experience four distinct seasons and the Wheel reflects that cycle, so at a crucial point in the class I always invite people to share what they are currently witnessing in nature. Sometimes I am met by blank looks if my students are firmly entrenched in urban life, but they soon get into the swing of looking around them with a little more curiosity. Many of the answers relate to what is visible in the city parks or gardens.

Yet as the Covid pandemic took hold and the classes went online, I noticed a change. My students were now coming from all over the world, so when I asked that same question, the answers began to fan out into something far more expansive. We began to hear how the forest-fire season began at Lammas, how Greenland got only four hours of daylight at midwinter, how the Spanish harvest oranges at autumn equinox, not just apples, and how the seasons were opposed in the southern hemisphere. As we celebrated midwinter, our southern hemisphere cousins were celebrating midsummer, and while we were celebrating spring equinox, they were at autumn equinox, and so on.

What is glorious about a modern-created, ancient-inspired practice is that it can adapt and expand to encompass whatever you are experiencing. There is no dogma that says in autumn you must celebrate the apple harvest if your local region doesn't produce apples, or if what you are seeing around you is the blooming of spring flowers. It makes little sense to celebrate the emerging hawthorn blossom at Beltane in May if it doesn't grow in your region. It's useful to understand where the practices come from, and what the symbolism is, but you can look for inspiration in nature wherever you happen to be in order to mark the festivals. The sabbats on the Wheel are therefore a blueprint, a guide, a map, but remember: the map is not the same as the land.

Likewise, the human experience has much in common wherever you are, so you will often find similar themes appearing in the seasonal practices of different cultures across the world. While pagans and Celts honour their ancestors at Samhain, in Mexico people mark Día de los Muertos; in Upper Egypt they visit their family graves; Christian faiths have All Hallows' or All Saints' Day; and others celebrate Halloween. Most of these festivals have existed in some form for centuries – across the world, there is a line of concordance that joins them all together, whether through the collective unconscious or some other means, in reverence of our ancestors and a remembrance of our dead.

One of the beauties of the Wheel of the Year is that it is cyclical, so you can begin marking it at any point. You don't have to wait for an appropriate 'beginning' to start celebrating the sabbats; you can do it right now. You just need a desire to align your own life more closely with the cycles of nature. Whether you're in a rural or more urban spot doesn't matter either. A quarter of a century in a major metropolis taught me that looking for the hidden paths and gardens, the window boxes and the tree-lined streets, paying closer attention to parks and waterways, can be more than enough.

Because of its cyclical nature, the Wheel of the Year also gives us a 'glass-half-full' perspective on human life. We are offered a chance to pause and reflect on our lives every six weeks – almost like being given a fresh start, a blank piece of paper. Not happy with the way your life has been going in the last segment? Great – you can start to make decisions that help bring about change and the next sabbat is the perfect moment to begin. Over time, I have also found a deepening of meaning that I hope you will begin to experience too. The Wheel is not just a circle, it's also a constantly moving spiral through life. Each turn of the solar year brings deeper nuances, and new insights.

As time has moved on since the emergence of Modern Paganism, the practice has grown and developed, and embellishments have been added by later practitioners. The Wheel has taken on other mythologies that are not always followed by the pagans who adhere to the original practices of Gardner and Nichols. This means you might encounter some differences between what you find on the internet and what I am sharing here. For example, you might have come across the story of the Oak King and the Holly King who do battle for dominion over the year – the Oak King takes the throne in the summer months, while come winter it is the turn of the Holly King. It is a nice story, but it was a much later addition to the Wheel in the 1970s when it travelled over to the United States. So too are the 'Celtic' names Ostara, Litha, Lughnasadh and Mabon, which were added in the 1980s to replace spring equinox, summer solstice, Lammas and autumn equinox. You will notice I don't use those terms here. This is not just because they came later, but because the thinking behind them is problematic in many ways. In the Wiccan community in the UK, many dislike those names with a passion, as they were added arbitrarily, some say for the sole reason of trying to make the Wheel sound more authentic. It is a personal choice, and you can choose to call the festivals whatever you like, but in this space I will guide you around the Wheel as it was taught to me, which is how Gerald Gardner and Ross Nichols originally conceived it.

As we are on the topic of language, there are a few terms I'll be using on our journey that might take you by surprise. The first of our knotty problems: Wicca. Wicca is a mystery tradition – it's not quite recognised as a religion in the UK – but nonetheless I identify as a Wiccan priestess, the title I was given when I was initiated into my coven. My training has been over twenty years long so far, but then, as my teacher is fond of telling me, 'In this life we all die beginners.'

It's not a life for everyone. There is a sense of vocation that comes with the title, and with that a calling. It also comes with a strong sense of the divine, and adherents recognise both the sacred feminine, the sacred masculine and every gender identity in between. Whether you are a monotheist or a pantheist, or an agnostic or an atheist, my world view may not be your world view, but what is important is that we all find our own way to connect to nature, the divine, and our own inner spiritual selves.

As this isn't a book about religion, but a book about connecting to nature and all that you find there, I invite you to substitute my terminology for yours. I have spent many years studying comparative religions and find fascination in all faiths. I am not here to convert you to paganism (it is a non-proselytising faith) and I respect all paths that help us to lead more fulfilling and happier lives, if we don't harm others in the process.

What this book *is* about is connecting to nature's cycles through these important pause points in the year. You'll find out about the festivals themselves – the myths, traditions, the spiritual and practical elements – and I'm also going to encourage you to think about what is going on in the natural world, to engage with the changing of the seasons at those times by going on walks or jotting down your observations in a journal. We have learned to separate ourselves

from the divine and from nature and the rest of the animal king-
dom, to see ourselves either as first in the food chain or last on the
list of priorities to attend to, and that means that some of us also
disrespect the natural world and our own divinity. By failing to see
what's holy in the everyday, and what is all around us, we have lost
all sense of the sacred.

I shall also encourage you to try your hand at several different
practical activities throughout the book where we make things, as
opposed to buying them. I practise lots of different crafts myself –
making soap, bath salts, candles and dabbling in needlecraft, though
I am spectacularly awful at sewing. Making your own items allows
you to pour some of yourself into these objects, giving them special
meaning, but also by engaging in particular activities or using particular ingredients that are associated with that time of the year, you
further connect with the Wheel.

Different times of year, for example, are 'ruled' by a particular
planet. This is based on an ancient system of planetary philosophy,
when it was thought that two luminaries (the sun and moon) and
five other planets revolved around the earth (Mercury, Venus, Mars,
Jupiter and Saturn). Each had their own set of characteristics and
healing qualities and the natural world was divided into things that
fall under the dominion of each one of the seven.

We still use this system of correspondences today. When we
create and make recipes – bath salts, balms, incenses, oils and brews
– we work with the list of correspondences for the planet we want
to call upon to help us in our endeavours. If I want to bring love, I
will work with Venus and I may choose to work with roses too. If
I want to encourage health and vitality, I work with the sun, and
perhaps orange or frankincense.

For each sabbat, I will give you the planetary ruler, the tarot
card and the astrological sign, as these inform the quality of that
sabbat. Also, each sabbat is given a cardinal compass point, which

relates to the direction with which the festival is associated. This is because, magically, we work in a circle and the Wheel is superimposed onto that magical space. As the Wheel moves onwards, we too turn to face the new orientation and place our altar in that position. And as we go, I will give you pointers about what all of these things represent, and it may be an area you want to explore a little further. If that's the case, check out my 'Further Reading' section at the back.

Throughout the book, and in each of the sabbats, I will also offer you a short ritual to follow to help give you a moment to pause, to connect to nature and reflect on your inner thoughts. This is really the point of the Wheel. Ritual helps all of us to mark transition points and to give them meaning. Ritual should not feel rehearsed. Try to let yourself go a little, allowing for spontaneity: that is where you will encounter the divine – and find a little magic.

Don't worry, I won't be teaching you to raise dark forces or practise *maleficium* – harmful magic. Despite centuries of accusations of Satanism, pagan witches don't worship the devil. You'll discover that I take a very down-to-earth view on magic, one that is about positive exchange with the universe and not about taking what you can get. Before you attempt to change the world, let's focus on changing your inner beliefs about what you can achieve – like an active form of prayer. Scott Cunningham, an American author who published many books on magical practice in the 1980s, once wrote:

> Magic is natural. It is a harmonious movement of energies to create needed change. If you wish to practise magic, all thoughts of it being paranormal or supernatural must be forgotten.

So you won't find the secret to magically disappearing and reappearing at will; what you will find are some seasonal spells to help you communicate with your unconscious self.

Connecting with and nurturing your inner self is to me one of the most important aspects of all of this. In our fast-paced modern lives, your sense of self-worth can plummet and self-care easily go out of the window. My twenty-plus years of working in the health and charity sector – my corner of which has been underpaid and underfunded for decades – has taught me how important it is to cherish yourself before you are able to support anyone else. The old cliché about putting on your own oxygen mask before you can help anyone else put on theirs rings true. Therefore, throughout the book I lean more into reconnecting us with our own sacred nature, rather than striving for the attainment of an external goal. I will also be encouraging you to be a little kinder to your inner self than you may be used to.

Each of the sabbats is presented with its themes or qualities, and the practical exercises are curated to help you bring more of that quality into your life. For example, at Yule we work towards finding hope, while at Beltane the theme is joy. At spring equinox we connect to your inspiration, and at midsummer we encounter the concept of sovereignty. I would encourage you to use this book partly as a resource that suggests how to live life in step with the seasons, but also as one that can help guide you on that spiritual journey inwards. While taking the time to work on yourself can feel a little like self-indulgence when you begin, it really isn't. It's a worthwhile investment that will yield riches for years to come.

So, then, back to the reason we are here – to nature's enchantment, and your nurturing guide to rediscovering and celebrating the Wheel of the Year. As I mentioned, you can start anywhere. I am going to start with Yule or midwinter, as this marks the 'birth of the sun', which seems as good a place as any to begin.

CHAPTER ONE
MIDWINTER OR YULE

21 DECEMBER (NORTHERN HEMISPHERE)
21 JUNE (SOUTHERN HEMISPHERE)

*The most ethereal forms belong to winter; hers is
the beauty the leaf has when substance and sap are
gone and only the frail white outline belongs. This is
the best time to learn the proportions of things.*

Mary Webb

THEMES: The shining light in the darkness, resting, birth
PLANET: Sun or Sol
DIRECTION: North
TAROT CARD: The Star
ASTROLOGY: Capricorn

If I were to ask you, 'What's happening in nature at midwinter?' you might be forgiven for thinking the answer to this question is 'Nothing much.' The trees are mostly bare, although some still hold on to crisp, dead leaves. Those trees have given into the impulse to just let go, whether gradually – like the planes that seem to drop one leaf at a time – or all at once, like the ash, in a seeming display of temper. They stand outlined against the winter skies, their naked branches on full display, their stretched silhouettes cast onto the brown earth by a low sun. Without the camouflage of the green canopy, we can see the true nature of these trees' central form, something that has been hidden since spring equinox, when the first smattering of new foliage began.

The earth is tilting on its axis, pointing those of us in the northern hemisphere away from the great solar orb, while at the other end of the planet our cousins are enjoying summer once more. The pavements and trails are imprinted with discarded and dead leaves that seem to melt into the stone. Leaves are also littering the gutters and the edges, and the process of turning all that matter into mulch is under way with each downpour and each set of footsteps through them – human or animal. This year's dead leaves will become the soil of a future year, enabling new growth and new life to emerge.

In winter, the physical path of the nature lover becomes dominated by form and by texture. The grass underfoot crunches with its coat of frosting; tree branches stretch out across the void. Even your breath takes on texture as it becomes visible in the cold air. The pathways become waterlogged with rain, and thick with mud. The pigs on the city farm frequently wear mud stockings – as do I! Scents are loamy and earthy. Colours are muted – browns and greens, clear blues and white, and black. The gnarly surface of the tree bark invites us to touch it, to trace the lines and shapes, sometimes coated in fine green moss, and embraced by boughs of ivy. Hedgerows now have only the jewels of their berries left on their bare branches, with little greenery remaining.

With so little that's new going on in the natural world (though that can be deceptive), it might surprise you that I am starting our journey through the Wheel of the Year with Yule, or midwinter. You might have heard too that it is Samhain on 31 October that is the Celtic new year. People therefore assume it must be the witches' new year too, but not all pagans identify as Celtic in their outlook. Marking a new-year point also assumes a linear measurement of time – the start and end of something – but the point of a wheel is that it keeps turning, spiralling through the seasons.

I have never been a fan of new year – all that pressure on us to go out and have a good time, to make new year's resolutions we shall all have broken by 3 January and replaced with a heady layer of self-loathing. If we shift the new-year point to October and Samhain, it's just moving the pressure. Instead, the Wheel gives us the opportunity to start afresh whenever we feel the need, to nurture ourselves whatever the time of year. To my mind, it really doesn't matter when new year is – every day can mark a beginning.

We start, therefore, with the darkest part of the year, and with the birth of the infant sun. Interesting thought that, don't you think? We have stumbled into the first of our worldwide archetypes – the birth of the sun/son god. Sound familiar? This has been a human preoccupation for millennia.

At this time of year, there are hundreds of memes online about who celebrated Christmas first – the pagans or the Christians. To me, this isn't the important question. The truth is a combination of considerations, depending on which aspect of Christmas you are talking about – the birth of Christ belongs to Christianity, but the birth of the sun/son, the midwifing of hope and the need to light up the darkest part of the year is global, and older. While Christmas as we know it is a much later reinvention that developed in the last two centuries, humans have been celebrating the midwinter point for thousands of years.

OUR ANCIENT ANCESTORS AT MIDWINTER

Many of the midwinter practices of our ancestors are shrouded in mystery, as they were based on oral traditions that were not written down. Nevertheless, while they didn't have access to the scientific knowledge we have today, they were able to observe the movement of the sun and to understand that something significant was happening, with the days becoming increasingly short between midsummer (summer solstice) and midwinter (winter solstice). The lengthening nights must have been just as poignant for our ancestors as they are today, if not more so, and one theory is that midwinter celebrations were held to encourage the sun to return before it disappeared completely. The word 'solstice' comes from the Latin and translates as 'the sun stands still', with this apparent stillness happening twice a year, though we don't know exactly what rituals were performed by the pre-Christian peoples of Britain and beyond to mark these moments.

What we do have is archaeological evidence of the significance of this time of year in the form of monuments – some of which date back to around 3000 BCE – sites such as Stonehenge in England, Newgrange and Knowth in Ireland, and Maeshowe in Orkney,

Scotland. Each of these sites was built with an alignment to the solstice sun in some way. At Newgrange, Maeshowe and Knowth the midwinter sunrise illuminates the passageway leading into the main chamber of the mounds there, while at Stonehenge the stones are aligned to frame the sunrise at midsummer and the sunset at midwinter. English Heritage, which now looks after the site at Stonehenge, suggests that winter solstice might have been most important to the people who built and worshipped at Stonehenge, as recent excavations reveal that huge feasts were held during those periods.

Even more remarkable is that this is not only a Celtic phenomenon. Several years ago, I was lucky enough to visit the Abu Simbel in Nubian Egypt, near the border with Sudan. This temple complex was built in the thirteenth century BCE by Rameses the Great and is accessible only by travelling a long distance into the desert. Rameses had it built at this far corner of his empire to make a bold statement about his conquest of the Nubian people at the battle of Kadesh, but also as a monument to his wife, Nefertari, who herself was Nubian.

There are two temples at Abu Simbel, the smaller of which is dedicated to the goddess Hathor, the patron deity of mothers, and to Nefertari and her children with Rameses. The larger of the two temples is dedicated to the sun god, Ra-Horakhty – a conflation of Ra and Horus – and to the pharaoh, Rameses.

The morning I visited, we had to set out from the Nubian city of Aswan before dawn had opened its eye to ensure we got to the temple complex before it got too hot and busy. Driving for hours through the desert in convoy for safety was a surreal experience (it's not only in movies that empty desert spaces become a haven for outlaws). The landscape rarely changes – just flat dusty ground to the horizon – until you reach the colossal temples themselves, which seem to rise out of the desert sand. What's so special about them, and the reason for me mentioning them here, is that the temple to Ra-Horakhty also has a small entranceway at the front, just like Maeshowe and Newgrange, sitting between the feet of four immense statues of Rameses. At sunrise on the winter solstice, the sun shines through this doorway, down a corridor lined with more statues, and lights up the holy shrine at the centre of the temple.

Elsewhere in time and space, our ancestors had other ways of celebrating the midwinter point. In ancient Rome, Sol Invictus ('Unconquered Sun') was marked on 25 December to celebrate the victory of the sun god Sol. This was followed by Saturnalia, another of the Roman midwinter festivals. Celebrated between 17 and 23 December, Saturnalia – despite being in praise of the god Saturn, who was not known for his cheery aspects – was famed for its light-hearted atmosphere, with all of the social norms of Roman society overturned. Public banquets were held, gifts were given, gambling was permitted, and it was a time of liberty for free people and slaves alike. One of the traditions was for masters to provide table service for their household staff, with a King of Saturnalia elected to organise the general games and jokes. Some of these customs were thought to have influenced the later development of Christmas traditions in western Europe, with the King of Saturnalia echoed in a 'Lord of Misrule' chosen to watch over the Christmas celebrations, which started to die away in Europe only with the rise of puritanism in the seventeenth century.

Other earlier traditions also made their way into the celebrations we still know and love today. In the pre-Christian eras, the Celtic Druids would sacrifice a white bull and decorate their spaces with mistletoe, until the early Church put a stop to this. While the bull might have faded into history, mistletoe did not. In the UK it is still traditional to kiss under the mistletoe, and in Sicily, 'Mistletoe is given as a gift to family and friends,' my Sicilian friend Angela tells me. 'It is hung behind the door to the house to ward off evil spirits and bring good luck in the new year. The old one is usually burned between Christmas and New Year.'

TRY THIS: DECORATING FOR MIDWINTER

In the pagan faiths, we do not have temples or religious houses in the way of most religions. We instead create our own sacred space in our everyday lives and in our homes. We begin by cleaning – sweeping away all the dust (metaphorical and literal) – and then cleansing the space, either by sprinkling a mixture of consecrated salt and water, or by burning incense. We also take a salt bath or shower prior to any ritual. According to the grimoires, or old books of magic, salt is an energy cleanser.

Next, we decorate the space with seasonal greenery or flowers, which we gather on the day of the ritual. We start to lower our voices as we dress the area, engaging fully with our movements. This way, we gradually step into a state of ritual consciousness – one that is quiet, contemplative and focused on everyone's individual relationship with the divine. Chatter and frivolity are reserved for after the ritual; otherwise it becomes too hard to make the transition. If you practise your rituals out in nature and can find that holy grail of being somewhere you won't be disturbed, you do not need to go through the process of cleaning and cleansing the space as it is already sacred.

At midwinter we decorate our homes with evergreen boughs – those precursors of the Christmas tree – just as our ancient ancestors did. When the world outside is grey and sad-looking, creating joy, light and colour indoors becomes ever more important to sustain us through the coldest, darkest part of the year. This decorating doesn't have to involve expensive baubles. Take a walk in nature and look carefully to see what is growing. In among the bare branches, you will encounter those evergreens that continue even through the 'dead' months of winter, symbolising the continuation of life: ivy, holly and fir trees; bay, rosemary and pine. These plants tend to be the twiggy, woody species. Please do make sure you are taking from a place of plenty and that you take no more than one or two sprigs from each plant. Always leave a gift for the birds and animals too – a handful of bird seed or some dried fruits.

Another option is to decorate your home in the way my Nan and Umpa did, very much inspired by post-war austerity. Instead of buying a Christmas tree, they would hang a pot plant with homemade ornaments. Buying them pre-loved would work well too, particularly if you can support your local charity shops.

One of my favourite midwinter traditions is to hang dried citrus rounds on the tree or in other places in the home. These little discs of golden fruit are not only in season in winter, but they are also evocative of their ruling planet, the sun. You can either buy dried orange slices or make your own. To do this, slice the citrus fruits thinly, lay the slices out on top of a clean dishcloth, and leave them on a warm radiator or in an airing cupboard for a few days. You could also follow the American tradition of stringing together garlands of popcorn and dried fruits, such as cranberries, though it might be far too tempting to eat them.

THE GREAT 'CHRISTMAS VERSUS YULE' DEBATE

The million-dollar question I am often asked is: 'Did the Christian Church appropriate a pagan festival?' My first answer is 'Probably', but my second is 'I don't think it matters.' Humans have been moving across the world, sharing and intermingling our cultures and traditions since our very beginnings. If you examine the pantheon of the Egyptian gods, for example, it's possible to see how they spread around the globe in different forms. The goddess Isis arose in Egypt but travelled across Europe, becoming conflated with other deities as she went – in Greece she was connected to Demeter; in Rome she was linked to Fortuna and Venus. She then travelled with the Roman army until temples were established in her name in what we today call London. The Christian Church, meanwhile, also came to England with the Roman Empire as early as the first century CE, but it wasn't until much later in the second century CE, when Emperor Constantine converted to Christianity, that the Church's own push towards evangelism really started to take off.

During the fourth century, Christianity became more visible in the British Isles, but it had not yet become the accepted religion of the people, who were still practising their own pagan forms of faith. One of the ways of making a new religion more attractive to the general population is to incorporate existing cultural festivals – which was very likely the case here.

When I tell my students they can continue celebrating Christmas if they choose to follow a more nature-based path, it's really coming from a standpoint of neutrality. It depends on what you see Christmas as celebrating. A Hindu friend marks Christmas with his children, not as a Christian holiday, but as the more secular version of the festival that many of their school friends celebrate too. Obviously, if you are a Christian celebrating the birth of Jesus, then you might not feel so neutral. Nevertheless, the origin of many of our 'Christmas' traditions is relatively recent and our 'traditions' are always evolving as we adopt aspects of other cultures. The Yule log, for example, was introduced to the British Isles in the eleventh century when portions of England were ruled by the Danish. While we primarily think of this as a chocolate treat, once upon a time it was an actual log, brought in from the woods and blessed before being placed in the fire to celebrate the birth of the winter sun. Christmas food was introduced around 1610, but the Christmas turkey wasn't on the agenda – alongside Christmas trees and Christmas cards – until the Victorian period. The concept of Santa Claus was Dutch in origin and taken to New Amsterdam – now the tip of Manhattan – by the European settlers, only to re-emerge in 1822 as Father Christmas in the by-then-renamed New York, before crossing the Atlantic back to Europe.

I am not advocating a homogenisation of different cultures – rather that each culture has much to teach us, and we should be open to them and to each other. Each religion has its own beautiful qualities, and if you shave away all the exterior fluff and look to their core, they ultimately lead to the same goal – a life that is connected to a spiritual force. As Sam, a treasured soul who used to tell me many wise things in my early years as a priestess, put it: 'Same bush, different way round it.'

FINDING REFUGE IN THE DARKNESS

You might have noticed that the name I give to our first segment of the Wheel of the Year is midwinter. Pagans also call this festival Yule, but I like 'midwinter' as it takes us away from the many different denominational views and returns us to the archetypal perspective. It also connects us directly to what the landscape is doing at this time – resting. Deciduous trees draw their growth down into their roots during the coldest months, while non-human animals such as bears, bats, hedgehogs, bees, wood frogs and some squirrels enter into a state of hibernation when the temperatures drop and food becomes scarce. Birds such as geese and swallows fly to warmer areas around the globe to escape the winter. While following the geese might be appealing, wintering is a crucial activity, giving the earth time to renew itself. And what is essential for other living things and the earth itself is usually vital for us too; it's just that we have forgotten about it in our disconnection from nature.

Why do we celebrate the darkest part of the year? This is a time when our primal fears awaken – the fear of an enchanted never-ending winter, or of what might lurk in the lengthening shadows, deep within the forests. For some of us, the darkness of winter also heralds an encroaching sadness and depression that comes from reduced vitamin D, which we usually glean from sunlight, and our level of serotonin – the hormone that helps us to maintain our mood, appetite and ability to sleep – can plummet with the temperatures. The lack of sunlight also affects our circadian rhythms, causing our body clock to falter. We might feel lethargic and irritable, craving sugary foods and gaining weight, which can then exacerbate the feelings of lethargy and lack of interest in the world. In the deepest, darkest part of winter, we are at our most vulnerable as we also face the darkness within. Our death rates also increase in winter.

Yet, times of darkness can also give us a moment of pause, and of refuge. Wintering invites us, at this time of hibernation, to strip back our own layers to see what lies beneath the masks that we present to the world. I would love you to think about the theme of this first turn of the Wheel as being 'you'. Who is the real you behind the carefully constructed persona? Who is it that you see in the mirror when you are tempted to look away so quickly? If you struggle to work this out, you could try sitting with a pen and two pieces of paper – one where you write down a list of the masks that you present to the world, and one where you write how you feel on the inside when you are wearing those masks. Sometimes it takes bravery to stand firm and look ourselves in the eye without flinching. This is the essence of 'naked', just like the deciduous trees – naked form, naked truth, naked self. (Don't worry, I am not going to make you stand unclothed in front of that mirror and non-judgementally look at the true nature of your own body, although you are welcome to try this.)

This dark, wintering period can be a nourishing time of rest and retreat for each of us. How might you foster that in your life? You might not be able to stop working, but you might choose to increase the amount of healthy, nourishing food you eat, or the number of duvet sessions you allow yourself. Remember, this is about healthy rest, nurturing and recharging. You might switch off the television and give yourself the gift of time to do the things that make you feel loved and cared for. When it feels as if the world might not be looking out for your well-being, make sure you fulfil this need for yourself. As self-help guru Wayne Dyer says, 'Don't equate your self-worth with how well you do things in life. You aren't what you do.' Let that sink in for a moment and, for this sabbat at least, just be.

While many of us might feel that shops filled with fairy lights and Christmas cards when we're barely past Samhain is a bit much, my friend Lizzie's take on this is that 'people need hope in the darkness' so that 'the earlier we can turn on some twinkly lights and give ourselves a sense of hope and magic, the better'. Light is such an essential part of well-being that sometimes I find it helpful to focus on how the sun is portrayed in our collective storytelling traditions. In the tarot, the sun card is said to represent health, hope, vitality, good fortune, happiness and the universe helping you forwards along your chosen path. It's not hard to see why light, and sunlight in particular, is so important to us. In circle we meditate on the light returning, bringing hope of a better future. If we can't have the sun, what harm is there in cheating a little by gathering together some twinkly fairy lights and candles?

One of my most memorable midwinter periods was one I had to spend alone. Events had conspired to keep me from my significant others, and so I used this time for deep reflection and long solitary walks. My diary notes that I saw my first kingfisher on Christmas

Eve – a flash of blue-green ahead of me along one of the city streams. It was so bright I thought I was imagining it, like something out of faerie. When all is muted, you can begin to see those things that you can't quite make out or could miss at more verdant times of the Wheel.

TRY THIS: OBSERVING THE BARE BONES OF WINTER

Next time you are on a walk in nature, choose a tree that you are particularly drawn towards and get to know it a little. This is a really grounding exercise, taking ourselves out of our heads and back into our bodies. You could do this at any time of year, but while the trees are bare in winter you have the opportunity to appreciate their unadorned form.

Take the time to *really* look at the tree. Are you able to identify it, even without the aid of leaves to show you the way? Notice the shape the bark makes as it runs down the surface of the trunk. Does it form in rivulets like the oak or in swirls like the sycamore? Is it slick like the holly or pitted like the poplar? What colour is it? Silver like the birch or reddened like the Scots pine? Does it flake away in your hands like the plane or the eucalyptus, or hold fast to the tree? Are there eyes in the trunk where smaller branches once were or is it smooth like the beech?

Feel the texture under your fingers. Sense, or imagine, the deep pulsing of life beneath your hands. Is there moss or fungi growing on the tree? Are there signs of insect life? Birds? What creatures make this tree their home? How does it feed them, nourish them, keep them safe?

Can you see obvious signs of human interference in the life of the tree? How old do you think it might be? Does it stand alone? Or as part of a group? Were they planted in a particular pattern – in a circle, or a line along a road or path – or is it more likely to have self-seeded?

What story do you think the tree would tell you if it could speak? Does it feel open and welcoming, or closed off and secretive?

When you are ready, thank the tree for its time – it's okay, you can do this silently – and perhaps leave it a token of your esteem: nuts for the creatures that make it their home, a cup of water tipped over its base for nourishment or a poem read out to show your appreciation. One of my personal favourites is 'In Praise of Trees' by Rabindranath Tagore, who wrote the poem in connection with an annual tree-planting festival that he founded in his home province. It closes with these lines:

> O profound,
> Silent tree, by restraining valour. With patience
> you revealed creative
> Power in its peaceful form. Thus we come
> To your shade to learn the art of peace,
> To hear the word of silence; weighed down
> With anxiety, we come to rest
> In your tranquil blue-green shade, to take
> Into our souls life rich, life ever . . .
> Man, whose life is in you, who is soothed
> By your cool shade, strengthened by your power,
> Adorned by your garland – O tree, friend
> Of man, dazed by your leafy flutesong
> I speak for him today as I make
> This verse-homage,
> As I dedicate this offering
> To you.

BEING A HUMAN LIGHTHOUSE

My mother collected strays. At one point it was the seven feral cats that lived around our house, each named after its most distinct-ive characteristic (Rickets and Piggy being personal favourites). At other times it was people, including Jim, who lived with us for six months while he went through the very painful and life-threatening process of recovering from his alcohol addiction (something not to be tried at home without medical assistance).

I attended a girl's school thirty miles away in our nearest city. At the end of each school day, I would put on my uniform beret and coat, and walk three streets to the hostel for 'naughty boys' where my mum worked. A stroll down the main high street with my mum always took time since homeless people, street drinkers and police officers alike all knew her by name and stopped to chat, while local people looked on, slightly aghast. Her other jobs involved facilitating a drop-in session for people struggling with alcohol addiction, run-ning a hostel for women visiting their loved ones in prison, prisoner resettlement following release, and training the local police in how to manage cases of domestic abuse.

You might think my mother would have been more renowned, but she wasn't. She simply went about her business, quietly and effectively, never asking for recognition.

As I grew to young adulthood, people would often ask me if I would follow in my mother's footsteps and I would always reply, 'No. I am going to be an actor.' I longed for the creative life and, in my heart of hearts, I knew I did not have the skill set required to follow my mum: I just could not switch off my sponge-like sense of empathy. Some of the situations my mother dealt with would make your hair curl, and I knew I would not be able to do what she did, and still be able to sleep at night.

The supreme irony is that life is never quite what you expect. Returning from another poorly paid acting job around the turn of the millennium, I took an assignment that no one else on the agency books wanted. Everyone else had turned it down. On my first morning at the drug-treatment drop-in, I announced to the amused team that they should not get used to me, as I was only staying for a month, thank you very much. That was over twenty years ago and I am still there, maintaining this work alongside my creative, spiritual and studying life, constantly learning.

If, like my mother, I can have a small part to play in being the collective lighthouse in somebody else's darkness, then I am fulfilling my oath of service and living by the values that my mother taught me, but also lighting my own darkness. You can't hold the lantern aloft without its light illuminating your path as well. Most honest social-care workers I know acknowledge that they do their jobs not only because they help support vulnerable people, but because it also makes them feel good. Coaches and tutors often say that you teach the subjects you need to learn the most. It is as if by helping others we are reminding ourselves of the value of those lessons, and relearning them for ourselves all over again. However, one thing I learned from my ever wise mother is that if you are going to shine the light for other people, you need to make sure you also keep your own oil supply filled. We do this by resting and refuelling with what inspires and nourishes us most. For me, that is quiet, reflective time in natural spaces that help bring me back to myself, clear my head, balance my emotions and propel me on to the next creative project. It's a delicate balance. In winter it can be tempting to push the focus to the interior life – indoors, in the warm – and neglect or turn away from the outside world, but the natural world still has lessons for us, even at its barest time.

It would be hugely disheartening to think we can't make a difference in the world. I truly believe that our actions are like little gusts of wind across the surface of a lake; as the breeze fans out with its own momentum, the ripples spread widely across the pool. As individuals, we might not be able to change the whole world, but we can at least, through service to our own communities, help change our own little corners of it. Without sounding too much like an info-mercial, or a trailer for that old Christmas favourite *It's a Wonderful Life*, whether your circles are small or large, midwinter is a time to connect with and reach out to our fellow human beings and those in need. This might be as small as stopping for a few moments to chat to the elderly man on the bus, who might not have had much human contact for days. Or it might be taking the time (and the £3) to buy that copy of *The Big Issue*.

What seems to you like a small gesture might be the one thing that changes the course of another person's life. If you're wondering what happened to Jim, the man who lived with us, he got well and for the last twenty-five years or so he has worked tirelessly in the Recovery movement, mentoring other people through the twelve-step programme. Ripples upon ripples upon ripples. Light upon light upon light.

TRY THIS: A RECIPE FOR SOLAR HEALING OIL

This recipe makes use of herbs that, according to the gri-moires, are under the dominion of the sun – with all the associations of healing and vitality that come with it. When you start to read through the list, you'll find that what counts as a solar herb is intuitive: they are the plants we have come to associate with the Mediterranean, such as olive, saffron and bay, and also the ones that look like the sun, such as oranges and orange blossom, chamomile, sunflower and dandelion. These solar herbs can be obtained from a good herbalist or online. If you live in a city, you will sometimes be able to find them in international supermarkets.

Frankincense pearls have a long history of use in sacred settings and are used to clear energetic blockages and cleanse the air of impurities. This aromatic resin was once burned in sickrooms as well as in temples, as it was believed it would expunge the air of any malaise. In the ancient world, the frankincense tree was grown only in the land of Punt, roughly corresponding to the modern coastline of Ethiopia, which amassed great wealth as this special tree sap was carried along the Frankincense Trail, a trade route very like the Silk Road from China. You can burn frankincense on a charcoal disc in a censer, just as they do in churches the world over, but we are going to infuse an oil with some of that lovely frankincense energy.

You will need:

* A teaspoon of frankincense pearls
* A cup of 'carrier' oil – if we want to be properly solar, then olive or sunflower oil would be appropriate, but any plain oil will do just as well
* Six drops of orange essential oil
* Six drops of neroli essential oil
* An empty bottle or clean glass jar to keep it in – do use recycled if you can.

Mix all the ingredients together, visualising yourself or the person you are making it for being full of health and energy, anchoring those thoughts to the oil.

Dab a few drops on your pulse points, to give yourself a little refresh, or you can use it to anoint candles, as in our midwinter ritual later in the chapter. Store your oil out of direct sunlight.

CELEBRATING MIDWINTER

In our witches' circle at the midwinter solstice, we take time to honour the darkness. With street lights and light pollution creeping in, it is increasingly difficult to find places of blackest night, but seeing the stars in the night sky in a place of true darkness is a poignant moment in our midwinter ritual. In other words, we do not deny the darkness; we embrace it.

We then light a single candle flame representing the 'rebirth' of the infant sun, inviting it back into our lives and celebrating the light that is to come. Modern witches and druids are not the first pagan faiths to celebrate this moment of rebirth. It's a concept that goes back millennia.

While midwinter represents the longest night – and therefore the shortest day – it arrives like a beacon of hope because we know from this point onwards, daylight hours will increase. My sister-in-law's late father, Frank, who spent much of his working life outdoors, said that each day there would be another six or so minutes of light. As a rule of thumb, that's good enough for me if you're living in the UK. It might vary slightly depending on your distance from the equator, so notice when the sun rises and sets each day where you are and how this slowly changes on the other side of midwinter.

It is worth noting here that our witches' circles tend to take place on the nearest weekend to the actual sabbat, and not always on the day itself. Modern life means travelling great distances to be reunited, so we often celebrate the sabbat with a group ritual and then have a separate, individual ritual on the day itself. You can be flexible in your approach throughout the Wheel of the Year: if you are not able to celebrate on the exact date, it does not mean you have failed.

Here are a few other ways you might choose to mark the midwinter:

- Buy a yellow votive candle and, using a pencil or cocktail stick, inscribe it with a wish that relates to new life, hope or a promise you are making to yourself. Light it and focus on that wish coming to fruition during the coming months.

- Look out at the night sky at midwinter. If you can, choose a clear night and go somewhere where there is minimal light pollution. Enjoy those pinpricks of light in the dark and imagine how tiny our earth is in relation to the vast cosmos.

- Think back on past tiny tender hopes you had in your heart, which you then nurtured into strong reality. How did you make that transition happen?

MIDWINTER LIGHT AROUND THE WORLD

In today's human tapestry, it's not only pagan faiths that mark this bringing of light and colour into the darkest of times. Most faiths the world over have a midwinter festival of some kind to celebrate the rebirth of the sun/son.

Judaism celebrates Hanukkah, the festival of lights that commemorates the rededication of the second temple of Jerusalem, following Hellenic attempts to conquer and convert the people. The war lasted three years, with the invading army desecrating the temple, the centre of Jewish religious life. When the siege ended in 164 BCE, the Maccabean leader of the freedom fighters ordered the temple to be cleansed and restored.

The Talmud describes how, on entering the temple to relight the everlasting light that was in the Holy of Holies, Judas Maccabeus found only one small jar of oil to light the lamp, enough to last only a day. Eight days would pass before more consecrated oil arrived, but in that time the light miraculously remained burning.

Today, as the candles on the Hanukkah menorah are lit all around the world during the eight days of Hanukkah, the people remember the miracle of the temple light and the rededication of their sacred temple. Like other midwinter festivals, Hanukkah is a joyous time, away from the restrictions of work, and also a sacred time, when the scriptures are read.

For their adherents, such festivals also become times of hope. Buddhism has Bodhi Day at the beginning of December, which celebrates Siddhartha achieving enlightenment. You can recognise those divine beings associated with the sun or with this sense of spiritual awakening as they often wear a visible solar disc around their heads. In Christian churches, a halo was placed around the head of the divine or the sacred beings (saints), while in ancient Egypt it was the solar disc that crowned the deities aligned to the sun. In Rome the god Mithras and in Greece Helios were also adorned with solar discs. Buddha too is often depicted with a surrounding crown of light.

What all of this tells us is that there is no right or wrong way to celebrate the midwinter point, whether for you it is as Yule, Christmas, Hanukkah, Kwanzaa or Saadeh.

TRY THIS: A RITUAL TO CELEBRATE MIDWINTER

If you can create a space in your home that you can make completely dark, that would be ideal. I want you to be able to experience that feeling of being in a velvet-black darkness. You might need to draw blinds and curtains, or cover windows with a large blanket or dark cloth to achieve this.

In the week leading up to your Yule ritual, I encourage you to start thinking about your blessings. What makes you grateful? What do you take for granted that other people might long for? Perhaps have a clear-out and give any unwanted items to your local charity shop. Buy a meal for someone who is homeless. Give from the heart and practise kindness.

In the ritual space, you will need:

* A gold or yellow candle
* Candle or tealight holders filled with candles and placed around your space
* Matches (long cook's matches are best) or a taper to avoid scorched fingers
* That bottle of solar oil you made earlier. Pour a little into an egg cup or a small dish so you have it to hand.
* A copy of a poem. I have chosen 'Winter Sunrise' by Walter Conrad, but if that doesn't float your boat, choose another that embodies those solar qualities – health, happiness, and success or the sense of rebirth. Have a look at Shakespeare's Sonnet 33, or the Orphic Hymn to Helios.
* A flat space to work on. In witches' circles we have an altar (I will talk more about altar spaces when we come to the spring equinox). A table or work surface is good if you want to remain standing and not be too low on the ground, or perhaps try a side table and a cushion if you want to kneel or sit on the floor for the ritual. For midwinter, we place our altar in the northern part of the room (if possible).
* If you can, decorate with a little seasonal greenery. This doesn't need to be vast amounts – a vase containing some evergreen twigs on your altar space could be enough.

Begin your ritual by lighting the tealights and candles except for the yellow or gold central one – candlelight always makes a space magical. Turn off all electrical lights so all you have is the candlelight.

Sit or stand for a moment and just focus on your breath as it moves in and out of your body at your natural pace.

Close your eyes and take three deep breaths, and with each breath bring your attention to the centre of yourself. Rather than stilling your thoughts artificially and getting in a tangle trying to keep them at bay, just allow your thoughts to drift on through your awareness like clouds in the sky on a windy day.

When you feel a sense of the stillness within, you can open your eyes and look around at the simple beauty of the space that you have created. Focus on where you are in the year – you might have been sad, ill or tired recently, perhaps subject to your fears more than usual at this time of the Wheel, or you may have been filled with hope. There is no right or wrong answer, there is only where you are right now, in this moment.

When you are ready, take the yellow candle in your hand, and anoint it with six dabs of the solar oil you have made. As you rub the oil onto the candle, think about your hopes for the coming weeks ahead. Place the candle in your candle holder on top of the altar space, but do not light it yet. Keep the matchbox handy, with one match on top of it, and be aware of where it is on the altar space.

At this point, you can acknowledge why you are in this space, by saying the following aloud or paraphrasing your own version:

> I have reached the moment of midwinter. My days have been shortening, leading me inwards to this point, leading me into darkness. This is the longest night, the darkest night of all. I have been afraid of the dark, cold and vulnerable. And yet, always a light in the darkness, a single flame to comfort me, and loved ones around me to cherish

me and hold me up when I need strength, to
love me when I cannot love myself, and light the
way for me when all I see is darkness. But for now,
I must enter into the darkest night, and honour
the time of winter from deep within myself, in this
time, and in this place.

When you are ready, move around the space and blow out
each of the candles, leaving the ones at the altar space until
last. When you are back at the altar, get yourself comfortable
and blow out the last flame.

Take a moment to pause and reflect on how the darkness feels. Do you have a sense of safety, or are you afraid of
what you cannot see? If fear rises, focus back on your
breath for a few more rounds. What does the dark make
you think about? Is it sleep? Death? Or is it a dark night sky
lit by starlight? Have you found silence in your darkened
room, or can you still hear the sounds of the world continuing outside?

For one final moment, allow yourself to bathe in that
darkness. Then, take the match and strike, lighting your
yellow candle while saying these words, or speaking from
your heart:

The sun has set on the shortest day, but the sun
will rise again, marking the journey back towards
the light part of the year. With this candle I honour
that light. With this flame, hope returns once more,
as I rejoin hands with my loved ones in the world,
and lead the way back towards the spring again.
The days will soon grow longer, and the sun will
return in strength.

Then, in honour of the birth of the infant sun, read your poem aloud.

Focus for a moment on the candle flame. At this point, you can begin to light all the other candles until the room is once more filled with illumination.

Think about those times you were in darkness in your life – physical or metaphorical. What led you through it? What lifted you? Who has been your lighthouse in your darkest times?

Give a moment of thanks for those people without whom we might have given up or stumbled. Then take a moment to think about those whom you have supported and the good you have done in the world. It is in those times of compassion that we can be somebody else's angel, even if it is just for a moment.

As a final declaration, say the following:

> May life continue to offer me those moments of
> clarity, warmth and opportunity. May I be aware
> of the world enough to see those moments when
> I can be of service, lighting the way and lifting the
> spirits of others. In word, and deed, may I use
> this life force wisely and to the good of all of us.
> In this moment, I dedicate myself to this path –
> to growing consciousness, and compassion. To
> increasing warmth and fellowship. To love.

When you are ready, you can give thanks to a deity of your choice and then leave the ritual space. When finishing a ritual, it's always a good idea to eat and drink something to remind your physical body of its part to play in this life, and to ground your energies back into the earth.

As you bring your midwinter celebration to a close, there is no need to end your period of rest and recuperation. Between now and our next turn on the Wheel, consider keeping a weekly date with yourself to practise some of those self-care rituals or place a light-filled picture on your altar or your workspace as a reminder of the importance of the returning light in your life, and of nurturing yourself. When we come round to Imbolc in February, you will then arrive refreshed and ready for the next adventure.

CHAPTER TWO

IMBOLC OR CANDLEMAS

1 FEBRUARY (NORTHERN HEMISPHERE)
1 AUGUST (SOUTHERN HEMISPHERE)

I wish it were spring in the world . . .
Ah come, come quickly, spring!
Come and lift us towards our culmination, we myriads;
we who have never flowered, like patient cactuses.
Come and lift us to our end, to blossom, bring us to our summer
we who are winter-weary in the winter of the world.

D. H. Lawrence

THEMES: Purification, dreams, imagination, the unconscious, youth
PLANET: Moon
DIRECTION: North-east
TAROT CARD: The Moon
ASTROLOGY: Aquarius

At each moment of pause throughout the Wheel of the Year, we tend to consider what has just passed before taking stock of the present and then turning our gaze ahead. As the first sabbat past Yule, Imbolc is on the cusp: winter is nearly over, but not quite. But it is not spring yet either, though the promise of the new season to come can be sensed all around us. The snowdrops, daffodils and crocuses are beginning to push their way up through the cold ground and the light layers of snow, but they are not yet revealing the full beauty of their hidden colours. They are still young, just green shoots – for now.

I'd love you to embrace Imbolc as a moment between times – a liminal space between seasons – that allows you to look back at the winter that has just passed; to let go of what is no longer serving you in the present and to look forward to what you would like to see grow within yourself and in your life over the coming weeks and months. This is a quiet time for observation, for introspection; by taking careful notice of what is happening within us and around us, we can prepare for the year ahead as the world gradually comes back to life. Our unconscious mind filters out a lot of the extraneous information we encounter in the world to prevent us from being overwhelmed, so sometimes we have to make a conscious effort to see what's going on around us.

Let's begin by noticing what is happening in the here and now. If I want to know what is happening in nature at a particular time of year, I always look to my journals. I've been a habitual diary-writer since the age of eleven, but I had to up my game when I began my PhD thesis on the writer Mary Webb, who was renowned for her microscopic observances of nature – to the extent that she could tell which flowers a bee had visited by the colour of the pollen on its legs. That year, I was still living in a studio flat on the outskirts of London, and every weekend I would take the bus to various bits of green and walk for as long as I could. Here's what I noticed around Imbolc:

> Imbolc seemed to have come earlier than usual to the city this year. On Christmas Day I was walking with my thick winter coat tied around my waist, dressed only in a T-shirt, sweating with the effort of pulling my feet out of the thick, viscous mud that sucked them down. The inexperienced oak saplings were already in leaf, while in Russell Square Gardens by the British Museum daffodils were already in bloom by New Year. But then mid-January brought with it a cold snap. The city had a blanket of snow wrapped tightly around her shoulders, and everything was held in stillness for just one day. There was no wind, so a layer of snow still clung tightly to the branches of the trees; even the birds were hushed. The snowfall didn't last. It will always be fleeting here, reminding us of the harsher winters of our childhood, tempting us to walk out in it and build snowmen, and then disappearing within the space of a heartbeat.

With a bit of extra walking from the suburbs, I was also able to access the countryside and the farmland that draped across north London. Getting out early enabled me to be the first pair of human feet to walk across the wide fields of white, feeling the compacted crunch beneath my feet. It was clean enough here to indulge in a favourite childhood pastime – eating handfuls of the ice plucked off the gateposts and fences, far above dog height. Yet, looking carefully, I could see the evidence of those who had been there before me: a fox dragging its feather-light breakfast back to its hole, a deer picking its way delicately along the slippery path, a solitary bird hopping its way across a wooden bench, perhaps surprised by the cold underfoot. The stillness and the quiet also enabled me to shock a few fellow walkers – a muntjac deer making its way across a snow-laden field, a golden pheasant flying out from the undergrowth ahead of me, crying out in irritation at being interrupted in its morning routine. Even the mere was frozen solid, the water preserved perfectly in feathered patterns of ice with its resident moorhens held captive in the one remaining liquid corner. The visiting lone swan that had been there over Christmas had departed for warmer waters, no doubt in search of companionship. The lakes and ponds of the city centre are far more populated by myriad bird life than this lonely outpost in Zone 5.

In the farmlands, ploughing would also begin soon after Imbolc. I used to love watching this process on my walks around the outskirts, where greenbelt farms would begin preparing the ground for planting a few weeks later. You could see the turning soil in progress, revealing the colour changes in thick bands across the fields, the black of the exposed winter earth churned into the rich brown soil underneath. When we begin by noticing this transitional time in nature, it also helps us to begin preparing our own metaphorical fields for planting. Some of that process involves a letting-go of what has gone before, to ensure that our new seeds of intention will land on fertile ground in the days ahead, clear of the energetic weeds of the past.

At midwinter, we travelled deeply, exploring the darkness without boundaries. With this new turn of the Wheel, we can seek the first visible signs of life in the outside world. Though the hawthorn is not yet in leaf, a very early blackthorn has burst into flower. What sparks of life can you see right now?

TRY THIS: A SILENT WALK

This exercise was taught to me by Victor, a fellow researcher when I was working on my PhD, during a week in which we focused on mindfulness as a tool. It's called the Silent Walk.

Pick a route that you know well. You can go alone or in a group, whichever you prefer. Walking in a group can still give you a sense of peace, while providing a background hum of safety. However, if you do go in a group, there is one rule to which you must all adhere – staying completely silent for the duration of the walk. If you are a solitary walker and are used to listening to music or podcasts when you walk, I would invite you to set those things aside for this exercise as they can be distracting.

When we take headphones out of our ears, or stop pouring forth the stream of consciousness in our heads to others, something interesting occurs. Your other senses can become heightened, and you will start to notice details you might previously have passed without seeing. You might find your thoughts tumble over each other to begin with, darting between various concerns that have been weighing on your mind. Try to let go of your worries, and instead focus on what you are seeing all around you in nature. You should find your mind stilling to a sense of calm, a resolute trust that will help you tackle whatever you're working through. By taking our minds off the problem, we allow our unconscious minds the space to find a solution.

Take a few moments to stop at a safe place and look around you. Use all five of your senses. What can you see?

What can you hear? What do you feel? What scents can you detect? What can you taste in the air? You might choose to focus on the details of a leaf or a branch, or a cloud formation. Notice what you are seeing without trying to make a value judgement. Does it remind you of anything? What thoughts does it trigger? In this in-between time in nature, what is happening? At first you might think not much, but if you look more closely you might start to notice the changes that are going on just below the surface. Green spears will be pushing their way out, in nature and in your own consciousness.

THE ROOTS OF IMBOLC

Imbolc has its roots in Celtic traditions, which means it is one of the truly 'old' holidays. The Church celebrates it as Candlemas, and in my line of Wicca it is still sometimes called this. In Christian traditions, Candlemas comes forty days after the birth of the infant Christ, and the Gospel of St Luke tells the story of the journey of the holy family to the temple at Jerusalem (the one we heard about at Yule). It was a time of ritual purification for the new mother Mary, following the birth of her child, and it was at the temple that Simeon first saw the infant Jesus and proclaimed him the light of the world – so Candlemas very much celebrates what it says on the tin.

In medieval times, people would process to the church to have their candles blessed and consecrated for the coming season, though during the Reformation this began to be seen as a superstitious act and was phased out. The festival would begin with fasting, with just bread and water the day before, followed by feasting on Candlemas itself – St Brigid's Day. St Brigid's Day was celebrated as far north as Shetland; on the Scottish borders, gorse fires would be kindled;

in Wales, Candlemas carols were sung door to door; and in Dorset, candles were given as gifts. Indeed, the name 'Britain' is thought to be a derivation of Brigid, or the tribe of the Brigantes who worshipped her, but she also leaves a trail of different place names in her wake across the UK and Europe: Brittany, Bridewell, Brent, Britannia, to name but a few. The feast of St Brigid is still marked by the Church today. But who was Brigid?

Brigid is both Celtic goddess and Christian saint, a nexus between the faiths. In Scotland she is Bride, to the Irish she is Brid, to the Welsh Ffraid. In the Church she is St Brigid of Kildaire, a woman who was born into the Druid population but later converted to Christianity when she heard St Patrick preaching. In the Celtic languages, her name translates as the fiery one, or the bright one – a solar goddess of many faces. The daughter of the Morrigan, the Celtic goddess of war and fate, and the sister of Ogma, who invented the Ogham alphabet, Bride is the patroness of healers, poets and seers. In other words, her bright spark is a creative one, inspiring creators to make their work, illuminating the future.

She is often represented by Brigid's Cross – an equilateral cross that would traditionally be woven out of reeds and hung above the lintels to protect the inhabitants of a home. In time, she became merged with Mary, the mother of Jesus.

She is, then, the lady that colours our associations of Imbolc, the flame that rekindles our fire as we return from the dark half of the year into light.

Yet, alongside this illuminating fire, Bride also rules the element of water, and specifically that of sacred springs. As the goddess of blacksmiths and the saint of holy wells, she becomes the Temperance card in the tarot – the blending of two converse elements to create a greater whole. In practice, this coming-together of water and fire joins inspiration to creativity, both qualities of the remarkable unconscious mind that we use together all the time.

Imbolc is the time at which such opposing – or complementary, depending on your perspective – elements sit side by side: fire and water; light and dark; life and death.

LOOKING BACK

While you might think it is better to keep the dustbin lid of your past very firmly shut, there is sometimes value in sifting through the events of your earlier life to glean and recycle the positive learnings. It can help you to lay old regrets to rest and pave the way for a more optimistic and different future. This is key because if we always meet new experiences with old attitudes and beliefs, we can keep repeating the same old traumas.

One of the most important things to take stock of properly is death – and the loss of those close to us. However far removed from nature the modern world might feel, we still experience more deaths in the colder seasons, making the quiet period of Imbolc a poignant time for reflection and remembrance. Loss in its many forms so often leaves us reeling, its ripples reaching us through many turns of the Wheel. I find myself returning to an old diary entry from a year that was particularly heavy with loss, and considering the effect it had had on me:

> This winter has brought me two funerals, both beloved teachers who helped to shape how I see the world. The first funeral was for my supervisor at university – a much respected writer who was taken far too soon by a brain tumour. Without him, I would not be on the path I am on now. That teacher brought me in from the cold, brushed the snow off my shoulders and gave me a mug of hot cocoa to warm myself. He leaves me in a much better place than he found me, with whole new worlds opening at my feet.

My second funeral was also for a teacher, my grandmother high priestess. She bewitched and carried me away during pathworkings – guided meditations – and wrote the most beautiful invocations to the gods. I recently found my notes from a talk she gave when I was in my fledgling days. I had been a solitary witch for several years but was then in need of a real-life teacher, and by luck wandered onto the path laid out by her and those she had taught.

This is the real meaning of lineage – the teachers who stand at our shoulders, speaking through us in unison. Voices from the past joining with ours, linking past, present and future, their legacy carried on forwards through us. Aside from my mother, these are the people who have shaped my adult life more than any others. They taught me how to live in the world, how to retain compassion and kindness, and how to question everything. And I am left wondering about my own legacy. What will I leave behind? How will I have shaped the world a little differently? Who will I have helped along the way?

THE GHOSTS OF WINTER'S PAST

Take some time to sit with your journal and consider the following questions:

- Who are the people of winters past – and the experiences – that shaped the way you are today, for the good?
- What was their legacy in your life?
- How might things have been different if it weren't for those experiences?
- Consider what you would like your legacy to be: what would it look like and how might you begin to move towards that?

Part of the reason for looking back over past events – and to those in whom we've placed our trust – is to help us face the future with less fear of the unknown. Therapists have been encouraging us for generations to undertake the deep 'shadow' work of exploring the parts of ourselves that speak of loss, that we dislike, or of which we're scared or disapprove, as it helps us to free ourselves from their power. There is something liberating about staring into the abyss of the soul and doing so without any preconceived notions of what we shall find there.

This kind of contemplation can sometimes be challenging and quite painful. We may think of the Wheel as being a turning circle, but in fact it is a spiral that takes us ever inwards as it revolves – this is not a path for the faint-hearted. Yet the rewards of such work are immense.

My hope for you in following this path is that you can come to a place where you can have a little more compassion for yourself. Even when you look back and perhaps think you made some mistakes, you might then accept that you were doing the best you could with the tools and knowledge you had.

If your world view of the divine is one of judgement and retribution, it can be hard to let go of the sense that we get what we deserve, but that view can drain you of all positive energy. When we sense the expanse of the universe as a loving force instead, we can start to let go of some of our fear of failure, giving ourselves a more nurturing base from which to build. I made this switch during a major life change, when my inner critic had been raging and saying cruel things. I asked myself if I would ever let someone else speak to me this way, and once I realised the answer was a most vehement 'no', the next logical conclusion was to make a change. I decided, going forwards, that my inner voice could use only kind words and a soothing tone.

You might not be able to change the universe, but if you start to change your corner of it, the effects will ripple outwards. Being clear that I would not tolerate cruelty on the inside went a long way in helping me to realise I didn't have to accept it on the outside either.

MAKING SPACE AND LETTING GO

It's not only the British Isles that celebrate the coming of spring at the beginning of February. The first of February also marks the Chinese new year, which is celebrated across other parts of southeast Asia as well, including Vietnam. Sophie, a tarot reader and yoga teacher whose father is Vietnamese, follows the traditions taught to her by her dad. 'First you must clean your house,' she says. 'You want to make space for the energy of the new year to come into.'

In the Japanese calendar, 2 or 3 February continues this theme. It is marked as Setsubun – the day before the beginning of spring. Setsubun is also associated with the new lunar year, chasing away the bad luck of the departing twelve months to allow for fresh luck to enter. In Japan, as in Vietnam, the home is ritually purified by the throwing out of soya or fortune beans while shouting, 'Devils out, fortunes in.' The family will then eat newly roasted soya beans to bring luck into their physical body. Houses are often decorated with holly leaves or sardine heads to ward off negative spirits. As Sophie says of the Chinese new year, 'Whatever you do now will set the tone for the next twelve months.' In the first few days, she makes a point of communicating with all the people she loves to ensure she sees them regularly throughout the year, as well as doing all the things she enjoys. This is a fortuitous time to make plans, so if you tried to do so in January and they fell away, this gives you another chance for a clean slate.

Among Hindus, Sikhs and Jains, 4 and 5 February are associated with Saraswati Puja, or Vasant Panchami. This is the festival of the goddess Saraswati, marking the beginning of preparation for spring, arriving in its fullness forty days later. People dress in

yellow, the colour associated with Saraswati. She, like Brid, is connected with creative energy in every form – knowledge, language,
music and the arts. Families mark the day by eating yellow foods
and encouraging their young children to write their first words, or
by gathering to read poetry and listen to music.

Around the world, Imbolc is a time of letting things go and
of creating an open and receptive space for inspiration. So let's
turn to an act of your own that is built around the idea of cleansing
past hurts.

TRY THIS: A SACRED SALT BATH TO CLEANSE YOU OF PAIN

As I mentioned in the midwinter chapter, in Western esoteri-
cism salt is seen as an energy cleanser, and some practitioners
choose to have a purification bath before celebrating a ritual.
Since the moon, the celestial body associated with Imbolc,
also governs the tides of the sea, I like to combine all these
ideas together to make a sacred salt bath. You can use this in
preparation for your Imbolc ritual or just when you are feeling
particularly frazzled or want to wash off the day.

With this practice, we are washing away any of the stag-
nancy or darkness we may have been shouldering, preparing
the ground for the new seeds of positivity and self-connection
that we will sow in the coming months. This is a fresh start.

If you add Epsom salt to the recipe, it has the added benefit of magnesium, which is renowned for soothing aching
muscles. I have added some words for you to say over the
salt and the water to give it a little dash of magic, but they are
not essential.

While you are preparing for the bath, spend a little
time with a pen and paper, giving yourself a period of nine

minutes to free-write in your journal all the things that have been bugging or hurting you – the things that are no longer serving you. (Yes, the nine minutes is significant, as nine is the number of the moon.) Set yourself a timer – you will be surprised how much steam you can let off. If you can get water-soluble or rice paper, even better, but normal paper will do. However, the ink in your pen does need to be water-soluble and not indelible.

For the recipe, you will need:

* ½ cup sea salt – I would recommend a finely ground salt, as it is easier to dissolve in water and is therefore less scratchy on your nether regions than sitting on big chunks of salt
* ¼ cup Epsom salt – this can be sourced from a good pharmacy but the recipe will work just fine if you are able to get hold of only sea salt.
* 1 tablespoon of bicarbonate of soda – usually to be found in the baking aisle of your local supermarket
* 9 drops of jasmine essential oil
* 9 jasmine blossoms (or if you don't want to buy a whole heap of jasmine flowers from a herbalist, you could cheat and add a jasmine green tea bag, but don't tell anyone I told you that)

With your fingers, mix together the salt, the bicarbonate and the Epsom salt in a bowl. As you do so, say the following words:

> I bless you, salt, that you may cleanse me of all
> negativity, and let all blessings of nature rain down
> upon me. Cleanse away all hurts and pain.

Then add the nine drops of jasmine essential oil, and the jasmine blossoms, and mix again with your hand. As you do, imagine floating in a calm sea, warming your body with the heat of the sun above you, and the soothing touch of the waters on your skin. When you are ready, run yourself a nice warm bath, and as the water is running, put your hand in the water and say:

> I cleanse you, spirit of water, that you may in turn
> cleanse my world of impurities and blockages that
> halt my way on the road back to myself. Wash away
> all hurts and pain.

When you are ready, tip the contents of the bowl into the water, and as you mix the water with your hand, say:

> I bless this water that it may wash away all hurts
> and pain. I call upon you [you can insert 'universe'
> or a deity's name of your choice here] and invoke
> you, that you may help me to continue on this jour-
> ney back to myself.

Collect a bottle full of the mixed water and put it to one side – it will come in handy later for space-clearing. Then get into the bath, lie back and soak, all the while imagining the sea that is carrying you onwards, under the light of the silvery moon, washing away all your hurts.

When you feel calm and refreshed, raise yourself out of the bath and gather together those pages of hurts you noted down. We are going to cast the pages into the water, which is why the ink must be water soluble. As you put each page under the surface of the water, watch the words dissolving, and say:

> I release those hurts, I release this pain, I forgive
> you, and I forgive myself. Water of life, take these
> words into your current and wash them on to the
> sea, the great mother of us all.

When you are ready, pull the plug and let the water drain away. Wring out the paper, which should now be unreadable, and recycle it.

The saltwater in the bottle you set aside can be used for purifying your spaces (and yourself). You can sprinkle it using your fingers or, if you prefer, use a sprig of something like rosemary. I keep a spray bottle handy in the house for those days when I need a little extra help.

NURTURING THE YEAR AHEAD

If you subscribe to the idea that each turn of the Wheel becomes dedicated to a new task, or a new goal, Imbolc is a time when the majority of the harvests have been reaped, and we are left fruitless once more. If the ground is not prepared – mulched and fed – at Imbolc, there will be less to gather in the harvests to come. And so we are invited to contemplate what gifts we might nurture in the coming months. What will you create as you look forwards? What will the work of this year be for you?

Turning to my Imbolc diary, you'll see this sense of looking ahead, of preparation and planning all around:

> The signs of new life are evident, even in the city. On my daily
> commute to work, I see a pair of herons, sitting side by side on
> a tree branch. Pairs of birds are visible everywhere: magpies
> and wood pigeons in the garden, robins in the hedgerow, crows
> in Lincoln's Inn Fields. Nesting, they collect their twigs and

moss to line their warm beds, homes for their eggs to dwell in, ready for hatching in the coming weeks. In my own life too I am planning the weeks ahead: meetings and projects at work, courses to squeeze in at university, talks to be given and visits to family members to reconnect to my own roots. The world is alive with the possibilities of what might be. It is time to decide my plans for this year and, like the clay soil beneath my feet, the future is there to be moulded and shaped, polished and then fired with the flame of creativity.

In our witches' circle at Imbolc, we focus on youthful endeavours – dreaming and contemplating. This enables us to imagine our future selves and achievements into existence before we begin those endeavours in the physical world, just as we did in our youth, when all things seemed possible.

We meditate on the Moon card of the tarot, representing layers of unconscious knowledge coming to the surface, light being shone on the underlying structures of our selves. It is connected to an intuitive power that releases the wild part of our nature, revealing hidden depths and truths. This can be unnerving, but also enables you to ascertain the state of play within yourself as you think about what you'd like the coming turns of the Wheel to look like for you.

YOUR UNCONSCIOUS SELF

The unconscious mind is the wellspring of so many things that bring you back to yourself and your desires. It is the source of our dreams, our imagination, it's the part of us that learns, and is the source of great power for all of us – not just witches! Imbolc is a wonderful time to allow some of this to bubble to the surface.

If you have spent any time in psychological, spiritual or thera-peutic circles, you may be aware already that you have two minds

– your conscious mind and your unconscious mind. Your conscious mind is the part that takes care of logic, reasoning and language, but the downside is that it can cope with only a finite amount of information at any one time before it runs into difficulty. The unconscious is the intuitive and creative part – the part of you that dreams, learns, imagines and that takes over when you enter a flow state, when you become so immersed in an activity you love that you lose all sense of time. This flow state is essential for our mental health – we feel happier and more creative when we reach it, and the work we produce is often better as well. The unconscious mind is where all the amazing change happens in your life. If you can change your unconscious patterns, you start to change your outer world.

The hard thing about working with your unconscious mind is that it is like working with a seven-year-old – it doesn't always listen to the language of logic and doesn't necessarily want to be told what to do. It prefers symbols, colours and sensory information as a way of communicating. It also loves stories and learns by imaginatively placing you in the centre of those tales, which is why fairy tales and storytelling are so alluring.

If you think you have that one straight in your head, then you are ready for me to introduce you to the third element – your higher self. This is the part of you, according to psychologists such as Carl Jung, that exists on a universal level – it connects to the divine, the collective unconscious and the part of you (if you believe in this) that exists through multiple lifetimes.

The slight complication between the three parts of you is the flow of information. The conscious mind and the unconscious mind can communicate with each other, but the unconscious (which takes over only during states of altered consciousness, such as dreaming, or when in flow) is the only part of you that can connect directly with the higher self. This means that communicating with the higher self is quite complex. Often, we get bits of information and insights that are 'downloaded' from the higher self to the unconscious while we are sleeping, or busy doing something else, but to access them we need to let the unconscious have its moment in the spotlight – either through meditation, flow states or quiet contemplation.

DREAM DIARY

One way of connecting to our unconscious mind, or our inner self, is to record the things that you are dreaming about. Most people will have come across the idea of keeping a dream diary, but if you struggle to keep one, do not despair. I can be quite a heavy sleeper, and the idea that I needed to train myself to write down my dreams before I forgot them was also a little beyond my skill or my inclination. If you can do this, feel free. If you can't, then consider keeping a waking dream diary, one where you allow yourself to go off with the fairies for a while and daydream.

Take yourself into nature with your notebook and a pen, and try to find somewhere you can sit quietly. Turn off your phone, as even a vibrating alert will be a distraction. Focus on one aspect in nature that draws your attention. It might be the way the leaves on the tree flutter in the breeze, the way that sunlight reflects on the ripples in the water, or it might be clouds scudding across the sky. If doing this out in nature is problematic for you, find a quiet spot at home and light a candle instead, and focus on the flame.

Allow yourself to relax, unfocus your gaze and unclench your jaw. Take three deep breaths and come to a place of stillness. Allow your imagination freedom to roam. What images come to mind? What impressions come to you? What is the thing you are focusing on – does it make you think of anything else? Let your thoughts wander. Write down any impressions you have.

If you do the sleeping version of this, you need to keep that notebook and pen by your bedside and write what you remember as soon as you wake; if you do the daydreaming version, just keep the notebook handy but don't focus too firmly on it.

The next stage is to 'decode' what your unconscious self is communicating. Sometimes dreams are a simple processing of whatever is going on in your life. If you have a big exam or presentation coming up, for example, you might have an anxiety dream (such as those where you get to work and realise you have forgotten to get dressed), but sometimes your dreams can be your unconscious communicating with you. I often wake up with a song in my head, and when I check the lyrics they tell me all I need to know, or sometimes it's a more obscure symbol. While you can google the secret meaning behind these symbols, I would encourage you to think about what this symbol, idea or feeling means to you first (as it's your unconscious). What childhood stories does it bring to mind? Who do you associate it with? With a little more doodling you can often uncover the hidden meaning yourself without the aid of a search engine. Obviously, you don't have to follow everything your unconscious suggests – but if it is a true reflection of your deepest inner self, why wouldn't you?

Other ways you might choose to mark Imbolc could include:

- Crafting candles – surprisingly, this is easier than you might think. You don't need expensive candle moulds and complicated equipment. I find soya wax is the easiest to use, as it gives a nice smooth finish. In my workshops we often make votive candles using paper coffee cups as the mould.
- Weaving a Bride's Cross using reeds – you can find some fabulous tutorials online.
- Visiting a spring and reading it a poem or a prayer in dedication.

TRY THIS: A RITUAL TO CELEBRATE IMBOLC

For this scrying ritual, I would encourage you to make use of that altar space we created back during our midwinter festival. We will be placing the altar in the north-eastern part of the room (if possible).

For this ritual, you will need:

* A white cloth
* Three white pillar candles
* Seasonal flowers to decorate your altar
* A bowl
* Some milk
* A small amount of washing-up liquid
* Some permanent ink or food colouring

Despite what people might think, scrying is not always about trying to see what will happen in the future – the future is not fixed (otherwise, why would we need free will?). However, scrying, like other forms of divination, is another good opportunity to connect to your unconscious, aiding your sense of what that 'something new' on the horizon might be.

In the week leading up to this ritual, spend some quiet time with yourself considering the questions that are troubling you right now. What challenges are you having? Are there any problems blocking your way? What actions do you need to take to move your new plans forward? What do you need to know in order to get to your end goal? If you find yourself a little stuck, that is what this ritual is for – to help move you towards something different.

Reflect on the humble spider. While we are sometimes taught to fear them, they are intensely creative beings. I often find my house is full of them when I need to get back in touch with my creativity. It's a reminder from my unconscious that I am not weaving my web as well as I could. On some mornings during Imbolc, when I walk out in nature, the hedges are coated in spiders' webs, gleaming in the frosty light of dawn. As you prepare for this ritual, think about what beautiful and strong web you might choose to weave around yourself.

For Imbolc, it is customary to put a white cloth over the altar, and to decorate it with three white candles. I like to use a church pillar candle, as you can relight them repeatedly and they last a long time, but dinner candles will work just as well. If you can gather a few snowdrops or early crocuses from your garden – rather than removing them from the wild – you might also like a posy of early spring flowers on the altar too.

I also place a bowl of milk on the altar, representing rich new life and nourishment. If you are vegan, you could substitute with a bowl of water with a tiny amount of washing-up liquid added (this holds the ink in a moving suspension in the water without dissolving completely). You will also need some permanent ink (not water-soluble this time) or food colouring, for the scrying.

It's worth me giving you a sense of what to expect here. When I first attended development courses at the College of Psychic Studies, I was convinced I had psychic constipation, as I couldn't 'see' anything. What was wrong was not my ability to intuit, but my expectations. Many people, like me, fail to scry 'effectively' in the beginning as they set their hopes very high. Working in this way won't create your very own personal Mirror of Galadriel, where you see a film show of what's coming to pass in the Shire. (Although if you can 'see' very clearly, don't talk yourself out of it.)

You are more likely to get an effective result by relaxing into the exercise and allowing your imagination to take free rein. Don't 'try' to see the future, just begin with a sense of curiosity and see what comes up for you. It might be gentle fleeting feelings. When I scry, I tend to enter a dialogue with my divine helpers, and I come away with a sense of knowing, of which I wasn't consciously aware when I began. The results of this exercise don't have to be dramatic or profound, or even portentous, but do keep your notebook to hand for any of the impressions that come to mind. Otherwise, when you return to full 'waking' consciousness, those impressions can be gone like traces of colour in a running stream.

Begin your ritual by preparing as we did before: clear and cleanse the space by burning a little incense or by sprinkling some of the saltwater bath mixture around – preferably before you have bathed in it! Cleanse yourself also – you can have that bath again if you choose.

When you are ready, dress in something comfortable, and if your altar is at coffee-table height, grab yourself a pillow or a cushion to sit on.

Light the first white candle, drop the lights down and get settled. Focus on your breath for a few rounds, bringing your thoughts to a place of stillness. When you feel ready, say these words aloud.

> Brid, heart of living flame
> Lover of the forge
> Sister of blessed springs
> Bringer of healing
> Mother of creativity
> Wellspring of words

> Bless me with your sight
> Lend your strength to walk the ways
> That lead me back to you
> And to myself

Bring the bowl of milk or water closer to you at this point and get the ink ready. Then light the next candle and say:

> The Wheel turns and a flame ignites in the dark
> Outside the frost still embraces the evergreen.
> The cold air bites at our fingers and toes
> Inside, away from the cold glass air,
> I turn within, reflecting.
> Ariadne spins her web and, like her,
> I am poised on the threads, listening for
>   movement,
> Waiting for the thaw that heralds the coming of
>   spring,
> But the stillness, the stillness.
> What would you have me know about now?

When you are ready, light the third candle, and place it closer to the bowl than the other two. Deposit three drops of ink into the water or milk. It's important to keep the bowl still at this point, so that the ink moves with the hidden currents in the liquid and by your gentle breath on its surface, but does not dissolve completely. Recite these words, inserting here whatever you want to know or to consider, even in broad terms:

> Thank you guides and helpers for showing me
> what I need to know about [—] right now.

Allow your imagination to roam freely around the images you are seeing in the moving ink. It is best to avoid writing anything down until after you have finished, because writing uses the conscious part of your brain, while scrying is done with your unconscious. But if you allow your thoughts to drift across the surface of the ink, it will leave you with a series of impressions, or perhaps one key line or feeling. For example, last time I did this exercise a favourite quote popped into my mind – 'have faith in life and trust in me' – which comes from a favourite Wiccan invocation, 'Charge of the God'. It reminded me to have courage in the process as it unfolded. What pops up for you might be a lyric or an image, or it might be a memory of a past event, long forgotten, which brings with it the realisation that you have been at this impasse before, as well as a sense of how you solved it.

When you feel that you have scried enough, or are beginning to get fidgety, say the following:

> May I step forward out of the darkness into the
>   growing light
> May my feet carry me along the threads of my
>   own web, sure-footed and steady
> Woven with the creative spark of divine
>   providence
> And so it is.

Then close your eyes, give thanks to Brid, or your own deity, or just the universe, and take another three deep breaths to bring yourself back, fully contained within your body. This is the time to write down your impressions before they drift away. Eat or drink something to earth yourself again – bread and cheese would be appropriate for Brid, along with a glass of milk, or just some plain old spring water.

As I hope you are starting to see, each sabbat not only helps us to work through a process of identifying and moving towards our goals – whether they're work-related or connected to much needed life changes – but it does so by reflecting nature back to us. After a time, you will have a sense of your life ineffably merging with the natural world, until they are indistinguishable – the outer world reflects patterns in your inner world, and vice versa. While Imbolc might be mistaken for an inactive time of year, most of the activity is happening beneath the surface as we prepare ourselves for new growth and the next stage of the year – the spring equinox.

CHAPTER THREE
SPRING EQUINOX

21 MARCH (NORTHERN HEMISPHERE)
21 SEPTEMBER (SOUTHERN HEMISPHERE)

I shall go into a hare,
With sorrow and sych and meickle care;
And I shall go in the Devil's name,
Ay while I come home again.

Extract from the Trial of Isobel Gowdie, 1662

THEMES: Balance, spring, communication, inspiration, the sacred non-binary
PLANET: Mercury
DIRECTION: East
TAROT CARD: The Magician
ASTROLOGY: Aries

Once upon a time, in a land not too far from this one, there lived a woman in a little house on the edge of the Great Wood. She lived all alone, but she wasn't lonely. She had the trees and her cat, and her books for company, and all the animals and birds that lived in the Great Wood. But while she was happy and contented, the people in the village nearby thought she was very odd. 'This can't be right,' the people whispered behind their hands when they saw her coming. 'A woman all alone? There must be something strange and unnatural about her. And she looks funny – she can't be more than thirty, and yet her hair is as white as snow.'

So, the stories about the woman grew, and each time a new story emerged, it was more elaborate and accusatory than the one before: 'She must be a witch, because didn't I see the farmer's wife visiting there not three months past? We all know she couldn't conceive, and now she is with child.' Which then went further: 'She turns herself into a hare after sunset, running around the fields with her mate.'

Then, one day, the squire was out hunting with his dogs. He was after the scent of a rare white hare that had been seen in this parish but had been eluding him for weeks. He was determined he would have that hare for his supper. At last, the pack caught the scent and were off, the squire spurring his horse on after them. Just ahead of him, he saw a white flash through the fields – the white hare! Yet, as fast as his horse could run, he could not catch up with that hare. They ran on and on through farmland, and into the wood. After a long while, the hare seemed to tire. She stopped to catch a breath and the squire saw his chance. Lifting his gun to his shoulder, he fired off a shot. But it seemed that he had missed, for the hare began running again.

Onwards, the chase resumed, but this time, it was slower. The squire must have grazed the hare with that last shot. The dogs, catching the scent of blood, bayed all the louder and ran after the hare with renewed strength. The hare, knowing she only had one chance left, bolted for the thicker trees, looking to find shelter there.

'Damn it,' thought the squire. 'Riding through those tangled woods will be much harder. I need to catch that hare now before I lame my horse.'

Just then he could see the lights of a cottage in the distance, the home of that strange woman about whom everyone whispered, which the hare was headed straight towards.

When he arrived at the little house, there was no sign of the hare. Come to think of it, there was no sign of the woman either. Just her black cat, watching him from the window with its yellow eyes, as it slowly washed its forepaw.

'Hello?' he called, as he pushed the door open. 'Is anybody at home?' Just then he heard a whimpering sound, like the noise of an injured animal, coming from the corner of the room behind a table. Feeling bolder as his eyes adjusted to the dusky light, the squire moved across the room, eager to discover his injured prey and finish it off. And there, in the corner of the room, stretched out across the floor, bleeding profusely from the gunshot wound in her hip, lay the woman.

Folklore is replete with such tales. At the time of the great fear of witches in western Europe and the USA, whisperings about witches who turned into hares or were accompanied by their hare familiars were common. On the frontispiece of Matthew Hopkins' infamous 1647 book *The Discovery of Witches*, among the woodcut drawings of Pyewacket and Vinegar Tom is the form of Sacke and Sugar, the rabbit-shaped daemon. Indeed, so infamous was the hare-and-witch combination that in the trial of Isobel Gowdie, a Scottish woman tried in 1662 for witchcraft, she was compelled – nay, coerced – to give details of the rhyme she would chant in order to transform into a hare, and then back again. 'I shall go into a hare, With sorrow and sych and meickle care,' she told her torturers.

Why have I started a new turn of the Wheel of the Year with all this talk of witches and hares? It is because the spring equinox – where we now find ourselves – is associated with the hare in its many shape-shifting forms. These creatures leap through our universal mythologies, with children's stories including those of Brer Rabbit (short for Brother Rabbit), the clever trickster who frequently outsmarts those who would try and control him. Brer Rabbit originated in parts of western Africa before travelling with the enslaved peoples to the West Indies and across to America, before being repackaged by white authors such as Joel Chandler Harris and Enid Blyton.

In Asia, folklore tells not of the man in the moon, but of the white hare in the moon, lighting up the night sky. In China the hare in the moon is said to pound medicine in a pestle and mortar, while in Japan he makes treats out of sweet rice. There, the hare is still seen as roguish, but he is also selfless and a friend to farmers. As a result, hares are protected. In ancient Egypt, the form of the hare became the hieroglyph that represented existence. Over time, hares have become not only a symbol of the moon, but also of femininity and fertility. This is largely due to the rapid gestation of their young, which grow for only forty-two days in the womb, arriving (unlike rabbits) fully haired and with their eyes wide open. Incredibly, the mother can conceive a kindle of leverets while still carrying another. It's perhaps no wonder then that the hare was sacred to the Greek goddess of love, Aphrodite.

In my corner of the globe, Devonshire churches are decorated year-round with a carved wooden disc showing the three Tinner's Rabbits – a trio of rabbits or hares that share an ear as they run in a never-ending circle. Each rabbit or hare is depicted as having two ears, and yet there are only three ears in the picture. The triple symbolism, like its close cousin the triskele, might relate to the holy trinity or the eternal cycles of life. Modern pagan interpretations lean into the Tinner's Rabbits as being a symbol of the divine feminine, since the triple moon goddess is also associated with the hare.

The qualities we give the hare, then, are many and varied: they are fleet of thought as well as foot, able to think their way out of any difficult situation. They bring light and life; transforming, transmuting.

Hares are ruled by the planet Mercury – the fastest-moving planet around the sun, named after the equally nimble Roman messenger god. And it is also Mercury that is the planetary influence for this sabbat, ruling over travel, banking and commerce, but also pickpockets and thieves. It brings us new ideas, inspiration and swift change, but can also give us a swift kick in the pants when we are not looking. Everything relating to mercurial energies is playful, naughty and comes with an edge of humour.

Added to all this, spring equinox is also associated with the tarot card of the Magician, a figure who stands at the altar with all the instruments he needs before him. As we step into this new season, this is our reminder that we also have everything we could ever need in our private toolboxes.

TRY THIS: THE MAGIC MIRACLE BOX

Spring equinox is all about inspiration and encouraging your unconscious mind to start focusing on the things you want to spring forth from the fertile soil of your life. This next exercise is intended to help you to do just that. The Magic Miracle Box is an expression of you, and works a bit like a vision board. It's there to help your unconscious mind, constantly running in the background, with the things you wish to achieve over the year, leaving your conscious mind free to go about your daily life.

You will need:

* A box (an old shoe box works well)
* Decorative wrapping paper
* A permanent marker pen
* Pictures to decorate the box that inspire you and make you think of success
* Slips of paper
* An inspirational collection of curiosities to place in the box – shells, pebbles, crystals, pine cones, ribbons and anything else that catches your eye.

Take a box, any old box. Decorate it as you choose. Mine is covered in gold wrapping paper and lined with cards from a favourite oracle deck, those representing Vision, Gratitude, Connection, Gift and Asking. I love the images on these cards, and the positivity of their messages. They are there to remind me that it is all right to ask for things, and to have goals, and desires. Without them we would remain stuck. However, don't feel you have to rush out and buy a deck especially; you could use any pictures or photographs that speak of success and gratitude to you.

On the outside of the box, write messages of appreciation, in expectation of the wonderful things it will bring. If you prefer to use a magical caveat, on the inside of the lid you can add: 'In accordance with my highest good, so it shall be.'

I then put crystals in my box, those associated with drawing good things or loving thoughts towards myself. I have a chunk of rose quartz, some green calcite, some malachite (to speed things up) and a few seashells I have picked up on beaches I love. You might choose stones, pine cones or coloured ribbons. The key with good spellcraft is to use what you are drawn towards – these objects and images are there to guide your unconscious magical mind, which communicates in pictures and feelings, not words.

Next, on small slips of paper, write down your goals for the year(s) ahead. They must be stated in the present tense and be positive – your unconscious mind doesn't understand negatives or the concept of time. For example, even though I am looking ahead, I might write: 'It is 15 February 2023 and I have just sent the final pages of my novel to my publisher.' We are laying out the threads that we'd like to see develop within the story of our lives.

For anyone who has encountered an annual performance appraisal, we are working with SMART goals (they should be Specific, Measurable, Achievable, Relevant and Time-bound). Despite their corporate associations, they are a great fit when it comes to harnessing the power of the unconscious and a good foundation for the effectiveness of any spell.

Once you have completed your goal-setting and popped the lid on your box, don't leave it in a corner somewhere to gather dust, as the energy will grow stale and stop moving.

It's good to check in with it from time to time and revisit your goals. Do they still hold true?

Once your goals have been achieved, you can either bury or burn the slips of paper with a thank you, before making a new set of goals.

SPRING EQUINOX IN NATURE

Spring equinox is on or around 21 March. As it is a natural event, and not just a calendar custom, the date varies slightly from year to year. The word 'equinox' comes from Latin – *aequalis* (equal) and *nox* (night). At spring equinox, we have reached the first of only two points in the year when we achieve a perfect balance of dark and light (the other being autumn equinox). In our more rural spaces, the ploughing that began at Imbolc has concluded, and the ground will now be planted for the harvests to come. Farmers are also readying themselves for some sleepless nights as the ewes are now lambing. In fact, any folk who have livestock will need to keep a close eye – no goat, horse or cow gives birth with our human agendas and diaries in mind.

During my childhood, the field outside our home would be busy on spring mornings with rabbit kittens taking their first steps in the open air. Meanwhile, hares start to emerge in Britain from their winter nests and become very active following a quiet winter. Like their namesake in *Alice's Adventures in Wonderland*, the long-eared, swift-running hares are bounding into a time of 'March madness'. If you're out in the fields, especially in the early morning or at sunset, you might also be lucky enough to spot hares 'boxing'. You might presume that these are the male hares competing in a show of masculine prowess, ready for mating. However, it's more likely that a reluctant female hare has decided it's time to see off an unwelcome suitor.

The birds are nesting too, laying clutches of eggs – a universal symbol for spring and the new life that will soon abound. Migratory birds are starting to travel back north, even though the weather is still quite fickle. If you walk in the woods, you might hear the cackle of a woodpecker in flight, and the ever talented song thrush holding forth from the treetops. When I walked in the woods around London, I had a particular song thrush I used to hear regularly, who included impressions of blackbirds and a buzzard in his song. In the insect population, the earliest butterflies – such as the comma butterfly – can be seen, alongside black-edged bee flies.

Elsewhere in the natural world, gardens are erupting into the colours of spring. The green spears of the daffodils are standing sentry, if not yet sprouting the yellow-paper flowers themselves, replacing the earlier snowdrops and crocuses of Imbolc. Primroses will also be opening in the hedgerows and the shaded spaces of the edges, with star-shaped wood anemone carpeting precious ancient woodland. The sap is rising in the trees, which are showing visible signs of life once more. Though most trees will not come back into leaf until mid- to late April, the blackthorn, the cherry and the plum have already burst into blossom. Signs of new growth are coming to every window box, and every city park. Blue skies are peaking between the gaps in the heavy grey cloud.

TRY THIS: JOURNALING TO FIND YOUR BALANCE

The themes that we're going to explore in our journal here relate to the sense of equilibrium at spring equinox. It's a chance to reconnect to yourself and recalibrate among all this sprightly activity.

This is a good opportunity to put pen to paper and see what comes out. Don't spend too much time thinking about this exercise, as it is one of those unconscious tasks. If you think too much, you will block yourself.

If the exercise starts making you feel anxious, pause, and take three deep breaths.

Here are a few questions you might consider as you think about your own story:

* Where do you need more steadiness in your life?
* Where have the scales been tipped too far to one side?
* What are the patches of shadow, and light, in your life?
* Where do you crave more freedom of expression?
* If you had a magic wand, and could miraculously fix the balance for yourself, what would that look like?
* What would you see, hear, smell, taste and feel when you reached that balance of both halves?
* Can you think of one thing you could do today to move in that direction? (If you get completely stuck, ask yourself: 'If I knew the answer, what would it be?')

EASTER AND OSTARA

Folklore and storytelling are an essential part of human life. Our unconscious minds love a story. So much so that when we immerse ourselves in our storytelling traditions, they place us at the centre of each tale, which is how we learn by association and through our imaginations. However, stories can sometimes take on a life of their own, leading us a merry dance.

At this point in the Wheel of the Year, the internet lights up with stories about how Easter, the Christian festival, took its name from the pagan festival of Eostre or Ostara, which itself was supposedly named for the Germanic goddess Eostre or Ostara, a deity associated with the coming of spring. The roots of this tale are usually traced back to the Venerable Bede, a Benedictine monk who lived in Northumbria in the eighth century. He claimed that the month we now call April was once known as Eosturmonath in honour of the goddess. For some time it was debated whether Bede had invented this figure, though there is now evidence of related lore that predates him. However, the word 'Easter' is more likely to be derived from the old German word for east (*eostarum*), which itself is thought to come from the Latin for 'dawn'.

Despite there being no evidence that the goddess Ostara was associated with the resurrection, eggs, rabbits or indeed hares – which is why you won't find mention of 'Happy Ostara' in this book – the story has really picked up steam over the centuries, influenced by supporters such as Jacob Grimm (he of fairy-tale fame). It has even had additional traction in more recent years with memes linking Ostara to the ancient Babylonian goddess of love and war, Ishtar, which they claim Constantine, the Christian emperor of Rome, changed into 'Easter'.

It's a lovely idea, but in reality Christians aren't marking the equinox and calling it Easter; they are celebrating the death and resurrection of Christ. And while we do now have Easter eggs and the Easter bunny, just to confuse things further, originally Easter did not involve the theme of fertility. The only important connection between the spring equinox and Easter is that the latter always takes place on the first full moon following the spring equinox – the moment at which the sun reaches a balance between the dark and light hours.

This does raise the question of why we need to invent a whole raft of folklore to make the Wheel appear older than it actually is or to justify a festival that is simply celebrating what is happening in nature. That's the inspiration our ancestors have been turning to since the beginning of human civilisation. The rituals themselves don't have to be ancient to be meaningful.

MAGICAL THEMES OF SPRING EQUINOX

What is happening magically at this time? In our witches' circle, we celebrate the awakening of the world, decorating the space with new spring flowers and greenery. The candle that we kindled at Imbolc has burst into flame. The great god Pan – the ancient Greek deity whose form is half human, half goat– is on the move again. Pan, like the hare, is a trickster – impulsive, full of trouble and associated with fertility and spring. Greek mythology is replete with tales of his gleeful shaggy-limbed antics at this time of the year, and as the son of the other trickster god, Mercury, Pan has a good pedigree for such associations.

This is a time to tend to the seedlings of the new ideas or projects that you began laying the ground for at Imbolc – to keep watering and feeding those things that you're hoping to achieve (or to give space to) in this cycle of the Wheel of the Year. This is the time to ensure that we are taking concrete steps towards our goals. Magic can grease the wheels, but you still need to put your back behind the machine and give it a good shove. For example, if learning a new skill is in the offing, sign up for a course and get started. If you want to be a photographer, start putting a plan in place for how you might exhibit your work. Emerge from your winter nest by making contact with people who can help you.

TRY THIS: THE BOOK OF INSPIRATION

Inspiration – a key theme for this turn of the Wheel – is another word we take from the ancient world. It is rooted in the Latin word *inspirare*, meaning 'breathe into'. This etymology starts to give us a range of clues about how inspiration might work (I often find when I am 'stuck', a few moments of focusing on my breath helps me to free myself), and I see a connection too with the divine force that animates us all and influences all that we create.

You will need:

* A folder or book that can have pages added or removed over time. I find a spring-form folder works well.
* Some sheets of loose paper to fit inside the folder
* Poems and pictures that inspire you
* A nice pen to write with

To feel inspiration, I find I have to go to a gallery, walk up a mountain or swim in a lake. I'm sure you'll have a handful of things that float your personal boat too. But sometimes we aren't able to embark on such ventures or we struggle to find the activity that will inspire us. For those days, I have my Book of Inspiration, something I was introduced to by my ever wise high priestess during my coven training. The Book of Inspiration is a black spring-back folder to which I can add or remove pages at will. Over time, I have filled it with my favourite poems, prayers, song lyrics, quotes and pictures. Whenever I need a boost, I spend some time with this special book and leaf through its pages, sometimes reading the poems aloud at my altar. It's my go-to place for the beginning of projects, or when I get a bit stuck.

I would encourage you to try this. It does need regular maintenance so it doesn't become stale, but you can add to it as you go. Begin with half a dozen or so pages and take it from there, building it over the coming weeks and months, even years.

SPRING AROUND THE WORLD
Elsewhere in the world, other festivals are in full bloom around the time of each hemisphere's spring equinox. In Japan, the Cherry

Blossom Festival takes place in Kyoto, while in India, Hindus celebrate Holi to welcome in the spring, as well as love, fertility and renewal. The dates of Holi vary each year, but it is renowned as the festival where a rainbow of coloured pigments is thrown, with each colour representing a different element – red for life and marriage, blue for divinity, green for nature.

In the Zoroastrian faith, an ancient Persian religion that dates back four thousand years and is still practised today in families of Iranian descent, Nowruz is celebrated on the spring equinox. In the month before, the home is spring-cleaned, making sure it is ready for a fresh start, and adherents take part in a thanksgiving ceremony called Jashan, led by priests. Ruby is a financial controller from London and marks Nowruz by setting up a *haft-seen* table in the home: an arrangement of seven items (*haft* means 'seven') that begin with the letter S (which is pronounced 'seen'). Each object has a special meaning, representing the seven creations of Ahura Mazda, the Zoroastrian godhead: fire, sky, water, earth, plants, animals and humans.

According to Ruby, 'This is a time for Zoroastrian families and friends to celebrate new beginnings with an abundance of food, drink and love, as winter changes into spring, when plants and flowers begin to grow and blossom, symbolising renewal, hope and joy.'

In eastern Europe, there is a tradition – like so many for the spring equinox – that focuses on the egg as a symbol of fertility and creation, but also protection. Pysanka, or Pisanki, are magical eggs, an ancient pagan custom that has survived the centuries and that are still fashioned across Ukraine, Russia, the Czech Republic, Romania, Slovakia and Poland. Pysanka translates as 'written egg' and they are made by a Pysanarka – a woman trained in the art of their creation.

Making the Pysanka involves preparatory rituals. The Pysanarka must collect the water for dyes from seven or nine special wells, or at a junction of three streams at 3 a.m., or by collecting snow in

March. This is so the water does not carry traces of any energy that might affect the outcome of the magical act. The dyes themselves are then created from roots, herbs and barks. Next, the Pysanarka must take a ritual purifying bath and dress in clothes that are completely new and clean. Finally, she can begin creating the Pysanka itself, first by inscribing molten wax on white eggshell to mark the areas she does not want to become dyed, and then by applying the dyes themselves. The colours are traditionally white, yellow, red and black, and inscribed with a special tool. As she prepares the Pysanka, the Pysanarka incants prayers or spells.

Pysanka are always given as gifts and never sold, and will either be buried in the fields to bring a good harvest, or placed on the altar inside the home to protect its inhabitants. If the egg explodes, then it means it has completed its work. They can be created at other times of the year as well, and there are many variations of this sort of egg-decorating in Slavic cultures, such as krashanka, which are hard-boiled rather than fertilised raw eggs and painted a single colour.

Perhaps unsurprisingly, the egg symbolism goes on and on. In Native American traditions and in China, creation myths tell of the universe springing from a great cosmic egg.

While eggs are a common theme during the spring equinox, there are a number of different ways you might choose to mark the spring equinox yourself:

- Paint a hard-boiled egg with food colouring on the morning of the spring equinox, quietly contemplating what you're hoping to develop in the year ahead. To seal the spell, eat the egg, thereby bringing the spell into yourself.
- Decorate your altar at home with some spring greenery – you can get some really affordable local spring flowers in the shops at this time.

- Spring cleaning – yes, it is actually a thing. At each sabbat I like to give my home a thorough clear-out to freshen up the energy.
- If you are musical, this is a perfect time for playing music. If not, simply enjoy someone else's efforts or have a little dance around your kitchen – a very spring equinox thing to do.
- Read *The Wind in the Willows*, but make sure it is the edition that contains the chapter entitled 'The Piper at the Gates of Dawn'. It's a beautiful story within the story as Mole and Rat encounter the Great God Pan out in nature.
- And yes, you can go right on and join in with the Easter egg buying and munching, if you want to!

TRY THIS: A RITUAL TO CELEBRATE SPRING EQUINOX

The themes of this sabbat are very evocative of the wakening of youth. While many of us will have gone beyond that stage in life, there is something to be said for getting in touch with a younger version of yourself. What served you then? What didn't serve? What patterns have you repeated through your life that have hindered your development? Why do we run those programmes still, and what can we do to set a new course for ourselves?

When our inner selves or our god(s) call(s) on us to undergo a transformation in our lives, it is rarely a comfortable experience. Instead, it is a process of faith – having faith that what we are transforming into will be better for us than what we were before; faith that the process of change will benefit us in the long run, even if we can't yet see the path ahead and where it will lead.

Spring equinox is the season of new growth, rebirth and change. Like the spring flowers, we need to break out of our green-paper coverings in order to bloom; like the mercurial hare, we need to be agile, fast and cunning.

In the week ahead of performing this ritual, think about what patterns you have mindlessly repeated throughout your life without question, and how things might be if you were brave enough to break out of them.

You will need:

* An altar space that we shall decorate during the ritual Place this in the eastern part of your room (if you can).
* An optional white cloth
* Spring flowers and greenery – enough to place some in a vase, and some around the surface of the altar during the ritual
* A basket or bowl of eggs – they don't have to be real eggs; you could use (vegan) chocolate eggs if you prefer.
* A yellow candle and a green candle. If you can't get these colours, substitute them with white candles.

Sit or stand for a moment at the empty altar space – this is your blank canvas.

If you are using a white altar cloth (it is not obligatory – some people prefer a naked altar space) place the cloth on it now. Otherwise just place both hands on the surface, and say:

> In the dance between dark and light
> Night yields to morning
> And the days gradually lengthen
> Bringing warmth again to our frozen bodies.
> Fleetingly we balance,
> Poised on the path between shadow and light.

The hare darts across our path, a flash of white
    against brown,
Bees stir to wakefulness,
Tumbling in delight in the newly opened spring
    flowers.

Begin to arrange the flowers on the altar space. As you do so, think about how you are painting your own blank canvas – the hope we sparked at Yule, the fertile space we created at Imbolc, is now springing to life with your inspiration.

As you place each flower or sprig of green, what new pattern are you laying down in your life? What are you changing around you? From the seeds you have planted, what green shoots have emerged? You are layering the spring flowers to welcome yourself back into your life with intention.

When the flowers are ready, place the candles among them, and bring the basket of eggs towards you.

Light the green candle. Take one of the eggs in your hand, and picture it representing an aspect of your new approach to life. Whisper a welcome to it. Carefully place it back into the basket and pick up another. What aspect of your life does this egg represent? Whisper a welcome to this one too. Take each egg in turn and repeat the process. When you have completed this, hold the basket to your heart, and say:

Spring, the season of soul growth.
Song, airy silence, a lively conversation.
No urgency about what is said or unsaid.
One long absorption with ground and sky,
What unfurls from within.
This morning, the flowers crack open
The earth's brown shell.

Place the basket down on the altar, and light the yellow candle. As you do so, picture your own flowers opening from within, turning your face to the warming sun that is now returning us to life after the long cold winter months.

At this time, I would invite you to make a promise of one thing you will do differently going forward in order to be kinder to yourself.

Perhaps it is changing your inner voice. If the voice you have tended to use has a harsh, critical tone, promise yourself that you will use only words of kindness from now on. Or perhaps you'll commit to one act of self-care each day. It doesn't have to be long-winded and can be as simple as taking the route to work that you prefer, even though it takes a little longer. Or maybe it is time to insist to your family that you have thirty minutes of quiet time for yourself each day, to sit at your altar or take a salt bath – whatever it is that you feel you need to help you on the next leg of the journey.

When you are oath-bound and ready, take three deep breaths, and end your ritual by saying:

> Once more I am roused from slumber by the
> piper at the gates of dawn and his spirits of
> mischief
> Wakening me to the forces that propel me
> forward through life,
> In me the hare becomes the creative spark,
> Spring will move into summer, as the sap rises in
> the forest
> And take me onwards to the next layer of my life
> Moving ever forward on the great Wheel of the
> Year.

Earth yourself by eating and drinking something you love. You can leave your altar in place for a few days to remind yourself of the vow or, if you prefer, take a photograph before you tidy it away and put it in your book of inspiration.

Over the coming days, if you find yourself slipping back into the old habits, don't be too critical. Just notice, and then remind yourself to move forward towards the next turn of the Wheel of the Year with kindness.

CHAPTER FOUR
MAY EVE OR BELTANE

30 APRIL/1 MAY (NORTHERN HEMISPHERE)
31 OCTOBER/1 NOVEMBER (SOUTHERN HEMISPHERE)

Unite and unite and let us all unite,
For summer is acome unto day,
And whither we are going we will all unite,
In the merry morning of May.

I warn you young men every one,
For summer is acome unto day,
To go to the green wood and fetch your May home,
In the merry morning of May . . .

Arise up, miss . . . all in your gown of green,
For summer is acome unto day,
You are as fine a lady as wait upon the Queen,
In the merry morning of May.

The Padstow May Night Song

THEMES: Joy, ecstasy, love and the sacred feminine
PLANET: Venus
DIRECTION: South-east
TAROT CARD: The Empress
ASTROLOGY: Taurus

If you are keeping a watchful eye on nature, you might have noticed that the world has just exploded in green. Within a matter of days, the hawthorn leaves have emerged, as have the leaves of the oaks and the rowans, with the plane trees following on behind, always the last to fan out. The parks are full of a rustling in the breeze once more. Just as we were beginning to wonder if the leaves would ever return this year, the natural world has taken root and opened outwards as Beltane comes upon us.

The sap that rose through the world in early spring has transformed the trees, just as it does our own bodies. In the Hindu faith, this is referred to as 'kundalini rising' – the form of divine feminine energy that rests in the root chakra at the base of our spines and, snake-like, coils upwards, bringing spiritual liberation and renewed energy.

The lambs are growing fatter in the fields, more confident as they spring about on all fours, and baby birds are starting to show signs of life in the nest. Dandelions, which first blossomed at spring equinox, bringing a much needed refuelling source for early pollinators, have bloomed across the sward and are at their peak; the grasslands are flush with daisies. In the woods, precious bluebells and wild garlic are flowering, nestled in the shadows of the oaks and beeches.

Remember that I mentioned how some of the festivals on our Wheel of the Year had ancient beginnings? Beltane is one of the genuinely ancient Celtic celebrations, marking the end of winter and the subsequent birth of summer – 30 April/1 May in the northern hemisphere and 31 October/1 November in the southern. (In earlier years of Wicca, the covens tended to celebrate May Eve – 30 April – but over time the celebrations have come to focus more on Beltane – 1 May). There's that lush sense of summer verdancy in the air, as butterflies with orange-tipped creamy wings emerge and the light changes, the days lengthening. A wet dog paddles happily in the stream, presenting me (as all dogs do) with that in-the-moment sense of pure joy, while hoverflies hang in the air, pretending to be bees.

While pagan traditions do not have one standardised book like other religions, and we tend to value orthopraxy over orthodoxy (prioritising conduct over faith), we do have one or two pieces of writing that are central to our practice. One of these is *The Charge of the Goddess*, a revered text with multiple authors, including Aleister Crowley, Gerald Gardner, Doreen Valiente and Charles Leland. Simply put, *The Charge* sets out the instructions of the goddess to her worshippers. It includes many favourite lines, but in the Valiente version there is this beautiful incantation:

> Let my worship be within the heart that rejoiceth, for behold: all acts of love and pleasure are my rituals. And therefore let there be beauty and strength, power and compassion, honour and humility, mirth and reverence within you.

My reason for quoting it here is that first line. Wiccans particularly refer to *The Charge* at Beltane, and perhaps that is not unexpected given the themes of this turn of the Wheel and the pleasures they bring. Beltane is ruled by the planet Venus, the energy that promotes love and pleasure, and also inspires the Empress tarot card, who comfortably sits amid luxury and plenty.

In this chapter, therefore, I want us to think about all the things you can do to get back in touch with your own sense of joy. We are so used to working hard and being responsible adults (mostly!) that sometimes we forget to engage with what brings us delight. Of course, there is the obvious physical or sexual dimension to this burgeoning time of year, but sometimes it helps if we build up to that. Before you can really experience joy with another person, we're going to ease into what connects you to that feeling in the first place.

TRY THIS: A RECIPE FOR ROSE AND HIBISCUS TEA

One of the simplest ways to work a little magic without anyone being any the wiser is with herbal teas or infusions. While a simple herbal tea bag can make a perfectly good cuppa, if I am working magically (as I do all the time) I prefer to use loose herbs. This recipe can be seen as a simple cup of rose and hibiscus tea, or you can approach it as a love spell to help you recover your joy. The choice is yours.

You will need:

* A tea pot or infuser
* Some dried rose petals
* Some dried hibiscus flowers
* Your favourite cup

For my teas, I have a lovely glass teapot, as I like to see the herbs, but any teapot will do. If you don't have a teapot, you can use a single cup infuser: just reduce the quantities down to a teaspoon of each herb.

Remember, intention is everything. With a little added intent, even a humble cup of tea can turn into a spell.

If you live in a city, pop to your nearest international or Middle Eastern supermarket and have a look in the tea or herb section – they often sell bags of loose rose petals and hibiscus flowers. If you are in an area that is less multicultural, you might need to find your nearest herbalist or order online.

You can experiment with your herbs too. Rose and hibiscus are both sacred to Venus. Rose on its own is lovely, but I really like including hibiscus as it does something magical when you add the water, starting deep purple, and then turning a shade of bright red.

To make your love tea, boil your kettle. While it is heating, imagine it placing a flame beneath your joy. Place seven hibiscus flowers in your teapot, along with seven pinches of rose – seven is the number sacred to Venus. Pour on the hot water and, as you do so, imagine the water becoming infused with all that joy and love. Stir the pot seven times in a clockwise direction.

Leave it to steep for seven minutes, then drink.

This tea is great for boosting your mood and sense of well-being, which can enhance your sense of joy and help you feel more connected to it. So, as you drink, contemplate a few lovely things you might do over the coming days and weeks to bring pleasure into your life.

HANDFASTING AND HAWTHORN

Traditional celebrations of Beltane or May Day were an appropriately joyous occasion, as people welcomed the return of summer and the warmer months. Celebrations involved 'Bringing in the May', decorating significant places such as the home, fishing boats and the church with blooming hawthorn boughs, otherwise known as May blossom or whitethorn. In some areas of the British Isles, it was said that if you found the sacred triangle of oak, ash and (haw)thorn, you'd have discovered the home of fairies, while in other areas hawthorn was hung as a protective amulet. Yet, when it comes to Beltane, the tree is connected with sex and death: the scent of the blossom on the midland hawthorn is reminiscent of putrefaction, while the common whitethorn is said to smell like sexual fluids. As you might imagine, given such associations, many of the Beltane ritual practices were discouraged by frowning puritans. In *The Stations of the Sun*, Ronald Hutton notes a grievance from the reforming Bishop of Lincoln around 1240, 'who complained to his archdeacons of priests who demeaned themselves by joining in games which they call the bringing-in of May'.

One of the 'nodding sage' stories about Beltane is that this was the first point of the year that it was warm enough to be out in the fields all night, which meant that nine months or so later Beltane babies were born. In reality, temperatures in the British Isles probably weren't warm enough for too much of this al fresco activity before midsummer.

Nevertheless, with energies rising, at some far-off point in our more agricultural past, when the nearest community might be far away on the other side of the hills, it was common at this time of year for young couples to come together and be 'handfasted' to one another at Beltane – a commitment that was said to last for a year and a day. This practice is thought to date back to 7000 BCE in our Celtic, Norse and English history and had the benefit of not requiring an officiant to oversee the ceremony. You just needed two people who wanted to make this pledge to one another, and it could be done in private, potentially with armfuls of whitethorn blossom as decoration – more of that bringing-in of the May. If at the end of that period the couple wished to stay together, then they might make it official, but otherwise they could go their separate ways.

Monarchs and religious leaders gradually eroded these traditions: it was felt that the frivolity of the general populace at large (including those demeaned priests) was inappropriate in the eyes of God. By the sixteenth century, the Church legislated the need for a priest, witnesses, vows and the reading of the wedding bans thirty days before an official ceremony. To this day, a pagan handfasting (now often officiated by a celebrant and involving a very literal binding of the hands with a cord or ribbon) is not legally recognised in the British Isles.

To welcome this turn of the Wheel of the Year with a little magical working of your own, you might:

- Gather the first dew on Beltane morning using a cloth that you then wring out into a small jar. Traditionally, this was said to bestow great beauty if it was used to wash the face.
- Bathe in a natural body of water, or dress a sacred spring with garlands of flowers, which is traditional on Beltane.
- Decorate your home or altar space with some may blossom, rowan or birch.
- Birth a new project for the year ahead (or a year and a day, if you want to be traditional).
- If your aim is to use the Wheel of the Year as a way of aligning your life with the patterns of nature where you are, then I would encourage you to pause at the very beginning of your summer season, take a look at the natural world and ask yourself, 'What is happening in nature where I am?'

LOVE AND LOSS, ECSTASY AND ACHE

The business of living is a messy and sometimes challenging thing. Our ancient ancestors in Egypt knew this when they represented their god Osiris as the god of death and life: his green face kindly, his arms crossed across his chest in what is now known as the Osiride position, holding the crook and the flail – the shepherd's guiding staff, and the scourge whose gift is pain. The message was that we can exist only with equal parts of love and loss, ecstasy and ache.

Beltane likewise sits opposite Samhain on the Wheel of the Year. In simple terms, they mirror each other, one heralding the start of summer; the other the beginning of winter. Like Osiris, they offer that balance between sex and death, love and grief. While Samhain is the time to honour our ancestors who have passed out of this life, Beltane is a time for celebrating the blending of egg and sperm that sparked us into being, in whatever context this occurred. Yet it also goes beyond simple biology. While in some circles the allegory of this process was reflected in the (heteronormative) coming-together of the god and the goddess, however *you* experience sexual pleasure in your life today is revered at Beltane as being vital to your well-being, both mental and physical.

Studies have shown that sexual activity boosts serotonin levels, which helps us to fight off depression, lifts our mood, and also plays a significant part in the bonds between partners. It also has a host of other physical benefits, lowering blood pressure, strengthening our muscles, and is thought to reduce the risk of heart disease, stroke and hypertension while bolstering the immune system. What's not to love? Nevertheless, Beltane is about the celebration of ecstasy in all its forms (not just sexual) and the myriad (consensual) ways that this can be experienced. As the writer and nature mystic Mary Webb wrote in 1911:

Beauty and Joy and Laughter are necessities of our being, and nature brims with them … The flawless days of May bring it – when big white clouds sail leisurely over the sky, when the 'burning bush' is in the height of its beauty, and white lilac is out, and purple lilac is breaking from the bud, and chestnut spires are lengthening, and the hawthorn will not be long. Out in the fresh, green world, where thrushes sing so madly, the sweets of the morning are waiting to be gathered. Joy rushes in with the rain-washed air, when you fling the window wide to the dawn and lean out into the clear purity before the light, listening to the early 'chuck-chuck' of the blackbird, watching the pulse of colour beat higher in the east.

TRY THIS: JOURNALING TO DISCOVER YOUR JOY

With the pressures of modern life, especially as an adult, it is sometimes easy to become separated from those things that bring us joy. Eventually, you may even feel as if you have no idea where to find it.

This is a variation on an exercise I was taught by one of my teachers, David Shephard, who runs The Performance Partnership, a company that specialises in training people to understand their unconscious mind better through neuro-linguistic programming (NLP).

The object of this exercise is to think back to the following periods in your life, up to the age you are now: 0–12 years; 13–17 years; 18–22 years; 23–30 years; 31–40 years; 41–50 years; 51–60 years and age 61 and upwards. For each period, list one accomplishment that gave you the greatest sense of joy – not what others thought was good, just what you loved.

Try not to spend too much time thinking – your unconscious mind will know the answer, even if you think you don't, and it's usually the first thing that pops into your head. And it doesn't have to be something that comes with a loud fanfare attached.

For each age range, ask yourself the following questions, and maybe write the answers in your notebook:

* What was the activity that gave you the greatest sense of joy?
* What did you actually do?
* Was the sense of joy connected to a specific element?
* What abilities did you demonstrate through your accomplishment?

You might begin to see a pattern emerging – it doesn't matter if it's in a very general sense. To give yourself a greater sense of the connecting threads, here are a few more questions to consider:

* Throughout your life, what sorts of activity have consistently produced the greatest sense of joy?
* What skills or abilities do you most like to engage with?
* What do you most like about yourself?
* What patterns, trends or consistencies do you observe in your answers so far?

It might be that you can't spot any sense of consistency, which is a pattern in itself: you might be someone who needs change and variety.

When I first did this exercise, I started to see that I was the most joyful when I allowed myself to be creative and have adventures, which means I can actively seek out those things and reframe the tasks I might not like quite so much with those qualities. (Ask me to do something routine but frame it as a creative adventure, and I will be right beside you doing it without complaint.)

Once you have identified the source of your joy, I would encourage you to incorporate this into your daily practice as much as you can.

THE QUEST FOR PERFECTION

A Muslim friend once told me the story of the architecture of mosques around the world. He said that when mosques are built, like all houses of faith they are designed to be beautiful and awe-inspiring. They represent not only the architect's vision of the divine, but the community's belief and love of God too. Inside they are decorated with the most beautiful geometric designs. However, each mosque holds a secret. Nestled in among all that incredible workmanship is one deliberate fault in each design – an imperfect tile, an off-centre window, or a mis-measured step – though you might be forgiven for never being able to spot it. Its purpose? To remind us that only the divine is perfect. In my own eyes, I am not sure even the divine tries for perfection, since nature is full of examples of the perfectly imperfect. Would a perfectly symmetrical tree or an animal with perfectly symmetrical markings be as beautiful as those we come across every day? Is it not the infinitesimal distortions of pitch and rhythm that give music its heart-stopping power? In fact, in studies where psychologists have looked at what people perceive as beautiful in other humans, it has been shown that perfectly symmetrical faces are never as attractive as slightly imperfect ones.

As someone who has had to balance my creative life around the 'day job' to make my life truly representative of the things I love, it means I have little time for seeking it myself. That doesn't mean I don't polish my work until it shines, but I also know that the quest for perfection can bring us up short and stop us in our tracks. When we are going for the perfect ten, we often miss the point and get stymied. If you have ever suffered from writer's block or something similar, you will remember the feeling of hopelessness and despair as you stare blankly at the page. It does not manifest itself only in the creative arts, but can extend to every area of our lives. This quest for perfection, then, blocks our path to the joy we can feel when we are doing what we love most.

In Wicca, we have an embodied view of our spiritual path. This means we are engaged with the full range of experiences we have in the physical life, both positive and negative. We celebrate our bodies, whatever form they take, as well as the delight and pain they bring. We also honour our 'imperfections', learning to look at ourselves (and the world around us) anew, with a sense of reverence. If our bodies are 'imperfect' (in the eyes of whom?) or causing us to blush, then our tribe will remind us that we are beautiful – or 'perfectly imperfect', as I like to think of it.

Given that we are all bombarded by images of the perfect bodies and the perfect lives we will never have – flawless skin, muscular and toned physiques (and this is fired at men and non-binary folk as well) – it can be quite the paradigm shift to be asking yourself to celebrate sexual freedom, ecstasy and joy. If you are feeling a slight unease at this point, bear with me on this one. I am taking you to a place where I hope you can be a little more forgiving of your human frailties.

If your upbringing taught you to be highly critical of your physicality, or of your own efforts, then celebrating your body and the physical exuberance and freedom it can bring you at Beltane can be quite challenging. Switching off that little voice in your head that reminds you of all your faults can be hard.

Shirley, a counsellor I know, poses this question to her clients: 'Whose voice is it that you hear when you listen to that sharp tone?' It might be the voice of a disapproving parent or another exacting figure, including online voices that encourage us to look or feel a certain way. Shirley tells me, 'Sometimes being mindful of that can be the first step to stilling that constant stream of criticism.'

Beltane invites us to step aside from perfection. It is as if our souls need reminding of the joy that exists in our bodies and our selves just as we are. If you can give yourself permission to experience this, if only for a moment, then you can remember what that feels like and steer your little boat towards it.

TRY THIS: AN APPLE SPELL FOR LOVE

Although apples were traditionally harvested around autumn equinox and stored as long as possible, in the modern era, they tend to be available all year round. They are sacred to the planet Venus and if you cut an apple across its hemisphere (horizontally across the middle) you will see that the seeds form a perfect five-pointed star shape, the same pattern Venus and Earth make when they both dance around our sun.

This idea for an apple spell is rooted in traditional spells and charms practised for centuries by the cunning folk, who were the historical precursors to modern witches. These wise ones were the people you would visit if you wanted your chickens to lay more eggs, or your cows to yield more milk. They were also the people you would visit to charm away your warts or relieve any spells that had been cast upon you by ill-meaning witches.

The traditional charms for love often involved quite bizarre activities, such as getting hold of a dried frog and secretly placing things under the bed of your intended. As we are not in the business of messing with people's free will or manipulating folk, Wiccans tend not to practise that kind of magic. Instead, I am going to suggest we focus on a spell for bringing in love in a more general sense, as opposed to focusing on a named person. If you have been on your own for a bit but are now ready to invite love back into your life in myriad ways then this spell can provide a wonderful springboard.

You will need:

* A whole apple – a nicely shaped one without bruises
* An apple corer
* A small piece of paper about the size of a small square sticky note
* Some green thread – preferably made from a natural fibre such as wool, cotton or hemp
* A green pen

Begin by sitting quietly for a few minutes, visualising what it is that you want to manifest. Really visualise it. If you want love to come into your life, what would it look like? What would you see, hear and feel if you felt really loved? What kinds of things would you want to be doing with your beloved?

When you have that picture in your mind, on the paper write your initials and a brief statement about the love you want to find – for example, 'healthy, happy love' or 'kind, generous love'. Keep visualising it as you write it down.

Then take the apple, and cut out the core using the corer, leaving a tube-shaped gap through the apple's centre from top to bottom. If it's not straight, don't worry. Retain all the pips from the core you've removed – we are going to need seven pips in total.

Next, roll the piece of paper into a small tube and slide it into the cored hole. Now, cut a long piece of your thread and wind it around the apple as if you're wrapping a parcel, crossing over at the bottom of the apple and tying in a bow at the stem end. This is to stop the paper falling out. As you tie the bow in the thread, say the words, 'A precious love I call to me, as I do will, so mote it be!'

When you are finished, go and find an outdoor space where you can bury the apple in the ground. Dig a hole deep enough to cover the apple but place the seven apple pips in the ground first with the apple on top. As you cover them over with the earth, recite the same words again. The spell is done.

Don't be tempted to dig the apple up again, and don't be tempted to keep going back to see if it has sprouted. If animals dig it up, don't worry at all – it has simply become part of the rich tapestry of life, and they have released the magic for you.

HISTORY AND FOLKLORE AT BELTANE

The word 'Beltane' means 'bright fire'. Before waves of people moved to urban centres, driven by the Industrial Revolution, large beacon fires were lit by our ancestors in high rural locations – blazing into the skies. In Ireland, a large fire was lit each Beltane on Uisneach Hill. From each tribal group, a representative would gather on the summit, in their hand a torch, which would then be lit from the central fire and returned to their home community. From this flame, each household would relight their hearth – linking each family and each group for the year ahead. Elsewhere, fires were lit in the fields and cattle driven between them to burn away impurities and protect against infections during the coming months.

Like so many traditions, these rituals were phased out in the Early Modern period, though the Bealtaine Fire Celebration of Uisneach Hill was revived in 2009 and now once again marks the end of winter and the beginning of summer. In Edinburgh, the practice of lighting Bale or Bel Fires has been reinvigorated in a 'dynamic reinterpretation and modernisation of an ancient Iron Age Celtic ritual'. This festival was restarted in 1988 with a small cast of performers, and an audience of about fifty people. Today it draws in an audience of thousands, with hundreds of performers. Huge Bale Fires are lit as people dance and revel in the birth of summer and the Goddess of May, representative of Mother Nature or Sovereignty, appears.

If you live in Germany, the Czech Republic, Estonia, Finland, the Netherlands or Sweden, you might be accustomed to celebrating Walpurgisnacht, or the Feast of St Walpurgis, on May Eve. All across Europe, fires are lit in commemoration of the English St Walpurga, who was born in my home county of Devon. She was a student of medicine and travelled as a missionary to Germany, where she founded a monastery and was instrumental in converting the population to Christianity. Her festival is thought to have deliberately coincided with the older rites of this time. She is also known as the saint who repels witchcraft, which means the fires that are now lit in her name also carry the secondary advantage of keeping witches away. Some countries go so far as to burn effigies of witches on the bonfire on this night. In Britain, 2 May was once referred to as the Eve of the Invention of the Cross, a day for gathering witchwood (rowan) twigs and forming them into a cross shape using red thread to guard against witchcraft. In Monmouthshire, this was done with May boughs instead of rowan, which feels perhaps a little ironic given its other associations, and hung over the front door of the house. If this all feels rather gloomy, I will offer you a reminder that May Morning is celebrated as a day of love.

Around the UK today, there are still some communities that celebrate Beltane, although the folk traditions within them have sometimes become separated from their original meanings. In Hastings there is a traditional May Day Procession with folk dressed as the Green Man, their faces painted green and covered in leaves.

The Green Man, or Jack-in-the-Green, is thought to date back to the period between 1300 and 1500, although in *The Stations of the Sun*, Ronald Hutton notes that he was likely to have been carved on late medieval churches as a demonic figure, not as a deity with an ancient connection to nature. Nonetheless, this figure's origins remain ambiguous and he has been embraced by many as a representative of rebirth and fertility. In Padstow, Cornwall, the celebration of ecstasy takes on a more subversive feel as the ''Obby 'Oss' takes to the streets. This sinister-looking, black-framed costume is paraded around the town, looking for young maidens to take beneath its mantle. When it catches one, they must pay a fine and be marked with a smudge of charcoal before they are set free.

The folk songs used in Beltane rituals can have a darker edge too, with allegorical tales of young women who have given in to sexual impulses only to die as a result. One such song is the 'Gay Green Gown', in which a woman is met in the woods by the devil, who says he will give her a beautiful dress if she will lie with him on the forest floor.

> The Proud lady she rode through the wood,
> And there in her way the wicked one stood
> Welcome ladye, light down, light down,
> I will give you a gay green gown
> T'will punish your pride
> For none who is bride,
> Wears such a gown,
> A gay green gown.

Realising her folly of having romped in the woods and given away her maidenhood for a grass-stained frock, she takes her own life. Our proud lady serves as a warning as to what might happen if you break the rules. Not only did she display sexual depravity in the eyes of the moralists (and therefore deserved her sticky end), she also demonstrates the worst thing a woman can be in the eyes of the patriarchy: she is proud and free. For years the colour green, symbolic of verdant nature, was associated with evil women, loose morals and the fae. There is a famous portrait from 1889 of the actress Ellen Terry dressed as Lady Macbeth, her fine green gown painted by John Singer Sargent as a warning.

Sharon Blackie, psychologist, mythologist and author of *If Women Rose Rooted* and *The Enchanted Life*, has written extensively on the native pre-Christian mythology of the Celtic nations. In the context of her work, we might see these tales of 'loose women' as a subversion of the role of the female deities in these older mythologies – punished, not celebrated, for their power. Blackie explains how in those nations, the creative, spiritual force behind the universe was inherently female. In this model of the universe, it was believed that the king would be chosen by the spirit of Sovereignty (one name for the feminine divine). On coronation, the king would enter a sacred marriage with Sovereignty, after which he was held to account for the well-being of the land and the tribe. 'Sovereignty's power was paramount,' writes Blackie:

> If the power she bestowed was abused, then we invited disaster. During the reign of a king favoured by the goddess, the land was fertile and prosperous, and the tribe was victorious in war. But if the king didn't match up to her expectations, he didn't last long. And what she expected more than anything was that the king, and through his example, the people, would cherish the land. So it was that the ancient rites of kingship in Ireland included a ceremonial marriage, the *banais ríghi*, between the king and the goddess of the land, and so fundamental was that idea to the Irish way of life that those rites lasted into the sixteenth century.

This seems a far cry from our constructs of power in the twenty-first century, but these ideas still permeate some of the folklore of Beltane – the May king and queen crowned at agricultural May fairs are perhaps the archetypal god and goddess. During my early days of Wicca, there was also the whispered notion of the Hieros Gamos – the sacred sexual union that was rumoured to take place in witches' circles on this night.

AROUND THE WORLD AT BELTANE

While Venus is the ruling planet of Beltane, the goddess Venus – whom the planet was named after – has many cousins and counterparts around the globe. This means if you look for religious or spiritual festivals celebrating the joy of life, love and ecstasy, you will be picking up on the Beltane energy wherever you are in the world.

In Hamamatsu in Japan, a kite festival originated hundreds of years ago when the local lord flew a kite to celebrate the birth of his son, and it soon became a popular tradition. It coincides with Golden Week (when four national holidays take place), beginning on 3 May (Constitution Memorial Day), through 4 May (Greenery Day, which celebrates the environment and nature), and culminating on 5 May with Children's Day, when families celebrate the birth of their boy children. (In case you are feeling a sense of dismay at the inequality, girl babies are celebrated on 3 March.)

In some parts of Great Britain, maypoles are still erected in town or village squares, with long ribbons attached to the top. Dancers then braid the ribbons around the pole as they weave around one another in formation, holding the ribbons as they go. This is hard to do without getting in a tangle and nowadays there is usually someone 'calling' the dance or teaching it in advance. Some say the maypole is symbolic of sex magic and was traditionally danced on May Eve by the young people in the village who had reached adolescence but were not yet married. The maypole was often made by the young men of the community and topped with a crown of flowers gathered by the young women, which was thought to symbolise womanhood. While various folklorists claim the may-pole as a phallic symbol, or at least a representation of one, Ronald Hutton, the historian who records much of pagan and ritual history, has found no evidence for this. As the sun rises on May Day, Morris teams also gather, this time to dance in the dawn dressed in colourful tabards, with bells tied to their ankles and carrying hankies or sticks. Today, teams such as the all-female Boss Morris offer a modern twist on this ritual with their striking attire and unique approach. The Morris is thought to have been introduced during the fifteenth century and came from Spain, France or Flanders, but we can only speculate on whether it was originally seen as a display of virility.

Meanwhile in India, World Laughter Day is an annual event intended to raise awareness of the essential nature of joy and laughter to our well-being. It might seem obvious, but sometimes we need to be reminded of the importance of simple concepts for our overall health. World Laughter Day was introduced by Dr Kataria in 1998 in Mumbai and is celebrated on the first Sunday of May. It also serves as a reminder that even if a particular practice is introduced as a modern reinvention of an older idea – like the Edinburgh Fire Festival or indeed the Wheel of the Year itself – it is no less significant.

TRY THIS: A RITUAL TO CELEBRATE BELTANE
To my mind, ritual is an essential part of living a mindful, embodied life in the embrace of nature, but it is one of those words that often strikes fear into the heart of the would-be

ritualist. It takes me back to my point about perfection, and how stymied we can be when we are seeking it.

While the dictionary might tell us that ritual is a solemn ceremony, I would wholeheartedly disagree. Ritual doesn't have to be a sombre affair, where you earnestly read aloud from a dusty old tome. Sometimes I prefer ritual to be spontaneous and that means it is sometimes filled with laughter. One of my best-remembered rituals in my coven was the time I got dizzy dancing around and fell over the altar. We have a saying in circle that ritual should be experienced with equal parts of mirth and reverence, and I think I embody that quite well.

This means that when I suggest a particular ritual, you shouldn't feel that you have to follow it word for word and carry out all the actions in a particular way. Allow your child-self to come out and play a little, and if something feels weird, change it up so you are comfortable.

A ritual can be as simple as making the rose and hibiscus tea I mentioned earlier in the chapter or as long and as involved as you like with memorised speeches and movements. It is about carrying out a particular action with an added layer of meaning, and while it is good to be reverent, feel free to be mirthful too.

For this ritual, you will need:

* Your altar to be placed in the south-eastern part of the room and decorated with a green or white cloth
* A green or white candle
* A cocktail stick or a pencil
* Some rose essential oil (available in most chemists or online)
* A cup of that rose and hibiscus tea (if you made it) or a glass of your favourite drink, be it champagne or fizzy

elderflower. Just make sure it is something that makes you feel good and is preferably a bit of a treat.

* Some food to eat once you have finished – if it's your favourite food, all the better.

If you can begin by having a bath with a handful of salt or your favourite bath salts thrown in, then please do. There is a handy recipe for a salt bath in chapter two – if you follow this, just substitute the jasmine flowers for rose petals. Ritual might not be earnest, but it is sacred, and by having a purifying bath first, you are marking out that time. If you listen to music at this point, make sure it is something uplifting, and not too dirgy or sad. 'Ode to Joy' by Beethoven could be a good place to start.

When you have bathed and feel ready, dress in something comfortable, preferably something that makes you feel good. Witches practise ritual in their birthday suits (yes, really!) and, in the spirit of embracing the joy of our bodies, Beltane might be a good time to try this. The object is to feel as calm, relaxed and happy as you can in your own skin – clothes or no clothes. It's really up to you.

When you are ready, sit or stand at your altar and take the unlit green candle in your hand. For a moment, focus your thoughts on the lush green of nature and how peaceful you feel in a green space. If you have a favourite deity or prayer you can call on it at this point. If you struggle with the concept of the divine, then you can call on your higher self or the inner unconscious mind inside you to help with this part.

I'd like to invite you to make a commitment to exploring your joy between Beltane and the next turn of the Wheel, midsummer. Make a promise to yourself to do one thing that brings you joy each day, whether it is dancing around the kitchen to your favourite song, or singing aloud in the shower; taking a nice bubble bath at the end of the day or going for a stroll around the park in your lunch break. These don't have to be large, ostentatious acts – small steps are often the best way to reach a larger goal.

When you are ready to make that commitment, take the pencil or cocktail stick, and carve your initials onto that candle, along with the word 'Joy', while repeating the words, 'I commit to my joy.' You can carve this as many times as you like (three or seven are always good numbers to choose, but once is fine if the candle is a small one).

Then drip seven drops of rose oil onto the candle and distribute them around the candle so it (and your hands) are coated in it. Breathe in the smell of the rose oil and, again, consider that commitment you are making to yourself and to your joy.

Light the candle and place it on a flat surface where you can focus on the flame for a few moments. As you contemplate it, you might like to read aloud a poem dedicated to joy. If you're unsure what to choose, take a look at 'Song of Myself' or 'Song of the Open Road' by Walt Whitman, 'Love' by William Wordsworth, or 'The Triumph of Life' by Percy Bysshe Shelley. If you prefer a female pen, then try 'The Summer Day' or 'The Sun' by Mary Oliver.

When you have read the poem, and are feeling that your resolve is set, say the words 'And so it is.' At this point it is best to let the candle burn completely down or, if you have to blow it out, say the words, 'As above, so below.' You are affirming that while the candle might be extinguished in this world (below), it is still burning in the world of your imagination and magic (above). You can then relight the candle for a few moments each day to remind you of that resolve over the coming days.

When you have finished, eat your favourite food and drink and relax. Bliss.

Try to keep returning to this sense of joy and pleasure as the Wheel turns onwards towards midsummer, where we'll be connecting with our well-being and sense of sovereignty.

CHAPTER FIVE
MIDSUMMER OR SUMMER SOLSTICE

21 JUNE (NORTHERN HEMISPHERE)
21 DECEMBER (SOUTHERN HEMISPHERE)

Oh, do not tell the priest our plight
For he would call it a sin
But we've been out in the woods all night, a-conjuring summer in
We bring you good news by word of mouth,
good news for cattle and corn
Sure as the sun come up from the south,
by Oak, and Ash, and Thorn

Sing Oak, and Ash, and Thorn, good sirs
All on a midsummer's morn
Surely we'll sing of no little thing
In Oak, and Ash, and Thorn

Rudyard Kipling/Peter Bellamy

THEMES: Health, healing, strength and sovereignty
PLANET: Sol
DIRECTION: South
TAROT CARD: The Sun
ASTROLOGY: Cancer

There's always a little confusion around the time of midsummer. People often wish me a 'Happy Midsummer' several days after it has been marked in the pagan calendar. This is because there is a disparity over dates: mainland Europe celebrates Midsummer Day on 24 June, but on the Wheel of the Year, midsummer is the summer solstice, which is on or around 21 June in the UK. In the pagan calendar, Beltane is the first day of summer, and the solstice falls exactly halfway between Beltane and Lammas, which marks the move into the autumn months. To confuse matters further, 21 June is the *first* day of the astronomical summer – not halfway through the season.

As feels very appropriate on a sunny day, our midsummer celebrations centre around the figure of the solar god archetype – from Sol and Apollo to Aten and Helios. Yule marked his birth; midsummer marks his coming to full strength.

You might have encountered references to 'Litha' at midsummer as an ancient Saxon name for this sabbat. This is one of a series of names that were added to the Wheel of the Year festivals in the 1970s to make them sound more authentically Celtic. In my tradition of Gardnerian Wicca, we still tend to call it midsummer – or summer solstice – in a joyfully straightforward way.

While we're on the subject of names, solstice is another word that comes from Latin – *solstitium*, describing the apparent stillness of the sun as it hangs steady in the sky for a few days. We have passed through that balance of equal sunlight and night-time hours that occurred at the equinox, and have reached the longest day – and therefore the shortest night – of the year.

The length of the day and night changes because the earth's rotational axis is tilted – and that is also what gives us our seasons. When the North Pole is tilted towards the sun, we in the northern hemisphere experience our longer, warmer summer days; during our winter it is the South Pole that is tilted towards the sun, shortening our days while lengthening those in the southern hemisphere. When midsummer falls in one, it is midwinter in the other.

You might wonder, though, why the temperature still tends to be quite mild around the time we're experiencing the most daylight hours. This is due to something called seasonal lag – the air temperature is dependent not just on the sun, but on the heat coming off the land and the oceans. It takes time for both, particularly the ocean, to warm up, which is why we tend to have our hottest days later in the season.

The further north or south of the equator, the more pronounced the changes in daylight hours become. If you travel at midsummer to those realms that are crossed by the polar circle – the northern-most points of Canada, Alaska, Iceland, Finland, Norway, Sweden, Denmark and Russia – you will experience the midnight sun, when the sun does not dip below the horizon at all. At midwinter, you'd experience the opposite – polar night, when the sun stays below the horizon all day.

Both sabbats are ruled by the planet Sol, so although midsummer is warmer, they share similar characteristics, giving midwinter a hint of health, happiness and success too.

Yet although midsummer is a point of celebration, bringing nature to its zenith, it also carries the bittersweet intensity of the days starting to get shorter, as the Wheel turns back towards the dark half of the year. This means there is always an element of 'make hay while the sun shines' to this sabbat.

TRY THIS: A MIDSUMMER INCENSE

One of the traditional ways to clear the old energy of the previous season is to burn incense, which is also one of the oldest ways to make an offering to the gods. Since midsummer is the second of the twin solar solstice festivals, we shall be using the same ingredients we had in the oil we made at midwinter.

To burn loose incense, you will need a roll of charcoal discs (available in international supermarkets or online) and a censer. Don't worry, you don't have to buy a special censer for this, you can create your own using an old mug that won't shatter when it gets hot. The mug version is quite practical as it has a handle for you to move it around safely.

Fill the mug up to about two centimetres below the brim with either earth, sand or salt. This is to prevent it from getting too hot when the charcoal disc is placed on top. First, let's make an incense.

You will need:

* A dessert spoon of frankincense pearls
* 6 drops of orange essential oil
* 1 bay leaf crushed up into small pieces
* A pinch of chamomile (you can take this out of a tea bag if you didn't buy the dried flowers for your midwinter oil)

Begin by grinding the bay leaves and chamomile flowers in a pestle and mortar, then add the pearls of frankincense resin, and finally the essential oil.

Light your charcoal disc and place it on top of your censer mug – you might want to use some kitchen tongs to do this as you need to turn the disc to a slight angle for the flame to reach it effectively. The disc will spark when lit; leave it until it turns grey. When ready to use, add a small pinch of the incense to the top of the warm charcoal – a little goes a long way.

It is a good idea to keep a window open for ventilation and to keep children and pets away from the incense smoke.

By using incense to clear out the old energy, we are preparing the way for an untainted new energy to come into the space – one that comes with a sense of your own sovereignty.

A MIDSUMMER'S NIGHT

If you have already read chapter one, you will understand something of the significance of the two solstices to our ancient ancestors, with evidence uncovered of ritual feasts and festivities. Sometimes that evidence will literally be beneath our feet, but with details lost in the layers of earth and time.

On the moor where I live, I often walk to a particular collection of Stone Age monuments and wonder what happened there before recorded history. There is a very tall standing stone that rises off to one side and can be seen for miles around. I think of it as the Old Man or Guardian. Immediately due north is a little stone circle and then a neat pair of double stone rows, with additional cists – or burial chambers – dotted around. With such obvious patterns in the placement of the stones, they clearly had a ritual significance for our forebears, but without the aid of a time machine (tsk!) it's hard to know whether they were placed this way because of ley lines, stellar constellations or some reason we can't comprehend.

Prehistoric stone rows, stone circles and standing stones are littered across the British Isles, other parts of Europe, Africa and the Middle East. If you can get to them, they are a worthy pilgrimage site for midsummer celebrations. Being in their presence not only makes you wonder how our ancestors felt during their solstice celebrations, but the considered placement of the stones, and their ability to withstand millennia of change, can be very inspiring. At the solstice, there is this sense of a hiatus – of time standing still for a moment – which can be something of a relief when our lives are otherwise in a state of constant transformation. When I stand next to the Old Man at midsummer, I can keep my angst about this change in perspective. To him, my lifetime is a tiny speck of dust that streaks across the heavens and is gone, but his existence lingers.

Outdoor celebrations are particularly poignant at midsummer: the long hours of daylight and balmier evenings bring a sense of mystical timelessness to this sabbat. One of my favourite historical portrayals of midsummer is that of one Mr William Shakespeare. Although you could argue that Shakespeare is a relative latecomer to the line-up of midsummer traditions, he based many of his plays on older folklore. The most obvious choice when it comes to this turn of the Wheel is *A Midsummer Night's Dream*.

The action takes place in a forest inhabited by fairies, who manipulate the visiting humans while playing out their own intrigues. Comprised of five dizzying subplots, this is a complex piece of storytelling, but the threads are intoxicating, with characters such as Oberon, the king of the fairies; Titania, his queen; Nick Bottom, the hapless weaver; and the mischievous Robin 'Puck' Goodfellow. Who among us doesn't remember Puck turning Bottom's head into that of a donkey, and Titania then falling in love with him under the spell of a love potion?

So well-loved is this literary offering that witches often look to tales of Robin Goodfellow and the dreamlike qualities of the woodland faerie-folk for inspiration at this time of year. The play's themes resonate – the sense of transformation, of timelessness and of possibility when we allow ourselves to become unfettered. The characters' journeys remind us that if we too step out of the confinement of city walls and into the forest, then we can enter an interstitial space where our day-to-day roles can be set aside like a costume while we explore what happens when we stop placing limitations on ourselves. The woodland, of course, becomes a space between the worlds, just like the witches' circle. Wheel of the Year sabbats are times of liminality – between the realms of the gods and humans; they allow us to step into our own imaginative woodland glen, and dance among the fae, if only for a short time. When we come back, we are often transformed in ways we could have only imagined while in the confines of our everyday lives.

While some midsummer traditions, such as gathering at sacred sites, have recorded ancient roots, the origins or meanings of others are cloudy and ambiguous. Several different traditions involve fires at midsummer, in both urban and rural locations across the British Isles, dating back to the sixteenth century and earlier. This might point to our northern European ancestry and a custom brought perhaps by the Viking raids and invasions between the eighth and eleventh centuries, but we don't truly know the original significance of the midsummer fires.

The pagan festival was also affected by the coming of Christianity, as it became absorbed into changing beliefs. Today, throughout the countries of northern Europe and beyond, the midsummer festival on 24 June is celebrated as the feast day of St John the Baptist. It remains one of the important events of the year, marked with bonfires, the weaving and wearing of flower crowns, and celebratory feasts – some of which might have been retained from those older festivals. In Iceland this night is celebrated as Jónsmessa, the time when cows can speak and selkies emerge from the cold waters of the North Atlantic – that sense of liminal, transformative energy again. Legend also states that if you sit at a crossroads where all four roads lead to a church, elves will try to tempt you away with food and other gifts.

For some of our most eccentric midsummer traditions, any spiritual or mystical origins have long been lost, if they existed at all.

In Devon, there was a tradition in the nineteenth century of setting fire to a cartwheel swathed in straw, which was then rolled down a hill. The hope was that it would roll towards the river – a safe bet since most of the valleys have a water course running through them – and the flames would be extinguished, signalling good luck for the community.

At Coopers Hill in Gloucestershire, onlookers hold their breath at the annual cheese-rolling event each midsummer. Great wheels of cheese are thrown down a very steep slope, reaching speeds of up to 70 miles per hour, and competitors then roll down after them in pursuit. While some folk try to claim that this custom has ancient pagan origins, it's more likely that it dates to the 1800s, signifying a riotous end to winter and the beginning of summer.

TRY THIS: WEAVING A MIDSUMMER CROWN

Midsummer is all about embracing possibility and stepping out of any self-imposed limitations to embrace your sovereignty. In my coven we often take a tip from our northern European cousins and weave midsummer crowns.

To make one, you will need to gather:

* Some strong but flexible seasonal foliage, such as willow withies (the long dangly bits on weeping willows)
* Seasonal flowers – do gather these sensibly, taking only what is abundant and not at risk
* Florist's, gardening or jewellery wire
* A good pair of secateurs

Begin by making the crown base. If using a dry woody plant, you might need to soak it in some warm water to make it more flexible, and then shape it around your head.

If you're using withies or some thinner foliage, weave strands of them together in a very rough plait. If you are using something sturdier, you may need only a single piece. It's nice to use something woody with leaves, to make the crown even more beautiful.

Secure the crown base with the wire, either by winding it all around or just at the join. We are not looking for perfection – in my group, the wonky bits are revered as they add to the charm, and if the crowns collapse during our festivities, it just adds to the freewheeling energy. There is a line in *The Charge of the Goddess* that reminds us that on this spiritual path 'mirth and reverence' are essential in equal quantities. I take that instruction to have fun very seriously.

Once you have the crown base ready, you can weave the summer flowers and blossoms into it, making sure to fill any gaps.

When your crown is finished, wear it with pride during your midsummer ritual or celebration, and then pop it on your altar to remind you of the beautiful possibilities before you.

CELEBRATING YOUR SOVEREIGNTY

While health and energy are central themes of the solar correspondences of this sabbat, well-being is not always something that is within our gift. In circle, we instead tend to mark the turning of the Wheel to midsummer by looking at the ways in which we can acknowledge our sovereignty.

This might be a moment to take out your journal and consider some of the things that *are* within your power:

- What can you control in your life?

- What is the source of your energy? And what drains it?
- What do you need to let go of (and how)?
- What intentions would you most like to set for this moment and the coming weeks ahead?

This could also be a moment to meditate on the Sun card in the tarot deck, and consider its themes of success, optimism and positivity.

The long summer days open up some lovely opportunities to celebrate this sabbat.

- In recent years it has become popular to go and watch the sun rise at a sacred site. You don't have to travel to Stonehenge or Abu Simbel to do this. Save on your carbon footprint, get up extra early and watch the sun rise wherever you are. (Or even watch one of the live-streamed events from Stonehenge if getting out is a challenge.)
- If you keep a dream diary, pay special attention to any dreams around this time: they might give you a hint about anything your unconscious mind wants you to know. Keep your dream diary close at hand when you go to sleep.
- Spending time in nature is always good for the soul, but while the weather is warm and dry, this is an especially beautiful time to get out and about in the woods or the heathland.
- Go for a picnic and share your favourite solar-inspired poetry with your companions. It might be Shakespeare's Sonnet 33, or Keats' 'Hymn to Apollo', or something less classical – the Beatles' 'Here Comes the Sun' is always a favourite.
- Cook a solar-inspired meal using Mediterranean flavours or foods from temperate climates, as they tend to fall under the auspices of the sun – think olives, olive oil, oranges, round loaves of bread and sun-dried tomatoes.

- Go swimming outdoors. Do take advice as to where to go, being wary of currents, pollution and unsafe places, and stick to well-known swimming spots on beaches and lakes. If you are in London, check out the ponds on Hampstead Heath, which are fabulous.

- Host a little solar-inspired ceremony or magical circle. A ritual can be as simple as each person bringing a favourite sovereignty- or solar-inspired poem to read aloud, followed by a shared meal. Keep it spontaneous and simple.

- Watch an outdoor performance – if there are any groups performing *A Midsummer Night's Dream*, all the better. If you are in Cornwall, check out the spectacular clifftop Minack Theatre for a magical experience overlooking the sea.

- Honour the spirit of midsummer by eating the foods that are in season in your part of the world – grow your own or choose foods that have been grown locally, not flown in from miles away.

- Have a barbecue in honour of the longest day. Honouring nature doesn't have to be mysterious or complicated; it can be doing the things you normally enjoy in summer but doing them mindfully, dedicating them to whichever solar deity you are most drawn towards.

TRY THIS: A RECIPE FOR DANDELION ORANGEADE

Dandelions have a long history of use in herbal medicine and are said to be good for all sorts of things. They are high in vitamins A and K, as well as antioxidants, and provide support in fighting infections and protecting your bones. In magical terms, these plants are uniquely placed under two planetary powers – the sun (when they are radiantly golden) and the moon (as dandelion clocks). As such, we make use of them in spells for health, success, well-being and the growth of energy. Perfect, then, as you commit to your own sovereignty and set an intention to allow yourself to shine a little more in the coming weeks and months.

If we think back to the idea of being in a state of flow (which we encountered at Imbolc), there is another idea I would like to introduce you to, that of *baraka*. *Baraka* is an Islamic concept that speaks to the idea of your life force (and your sovereignty) streaming into the things you touch and focus on. In its simplest terms, this is how magic and creativity work. If you can place your attention on a given aim and lose yourself in the wonder of the tasks you are carrying out – whether you are creating something intricate or simply stirring a jug of orangeade – then you are starting to apply magic. As the author Denise Linn says, 'Where intention goes, energy flows.'

For this recipe, you will need:

* 12 dandelion blossoms
* 6 oranges
* One large jug
* Boiled water (about 2 litres)
* Honey to taste

Gather the dandelion blossoms as early in the day as possible. Remember to pick them away from high-traffic areas and in places that dogs are unlikely to have watered (for example, not around tall standing things like trees or lamp posts). These flowers are an important source of pollen for bees, so don't strip them all back – make sure there are plenty left for nature.

Take them home, wash them thoroughly and remove the stems from the flowers. When the water has boiled, allow it to cool slightly, so as not to scald the dandelions. Put the flower blossoms in your jug, and pour over about one-third of the water, placing a saucer or a plate over the top, to ensure the steam stays in. You don't want all that dandelion goodness to evaporate. While this is cooling, juice your oranges, and add to the dandelion infusion. When the water has cooled a little more, take the saucer off the jug and stir the mixture, all the while holding your intention in mind to ensure that as much of your *baraka* as possible is imprinted on the spell. If you are making this as a group, make sure that everyone involved has a good stir to add their intention too.

When the stirring is done, top up the jug with the rest of the water, and pop the saucer back on top. Leave it to stand for another hour, if you can wait that long. Then strain the mixture, compost the discarded flower heads, and pour into glasses. Sweeten with honey to taste, or if you prefer the vegan option, sweeten with raw cane sugar.

MIDSUMMER IN NATURE

Clearly, for any midsummer solstice celebrations to take place at sunrise, you need to be out of bed much earlier than you do to mark midwinter. Nevertheless, there is something magical about being up before the sun. It has long been my routine to wake before sunrise to write (the perils of balancing a day job with a passion) and during lockdowns in the city during the Covid pandemic, I began walking at that time too to avoid crowds. Some of my most magical encounters with the natural world have occurred long 'before the day belongs to man', as Mary Webb put it. If you get out early enough, you might encounter a kingfisher catching its food on the river, a buzzard pausing on the ground long enough to devour its breakfast, or a deer making its way, fleet-footed, through the woods. All of these sightings are rare, but more likely to happen during the first moments of daylight, before other folk are up and about.

My nature diaries for this month record:

a heron in flight, its form reminding me so much of the illustrations of pterodactyls, especially when greeted by one of their hoarse cries across the treetops. Three vast grey-skinned carp swimming up to me, with hundreds of golden baby fish breaking the surface of the water. Bees patiently gathering nectar from an abundance of wildflowers in the meadow – knapweed, betony, cow parsley, buttercup and clover. Butterflies flitting from branch to flower, camera-shy and fleeting. Bramble blossom and green as far as the eye can see. In the gardens, lilies, heavy-scented roses, lavender spears. The first foxglove, with a fat bumblebee tumbling in its blossom in ecstasy.

Like nature, we must learn when to expel our energy in the act of creation and when to rest – to be still, silent and watchful, like the birds preparing for their summer moult, and take the chance to bathe in the sunshine. While the turning of the year back into the dark half can feel a little daunting and sad, for some it can be a relief to step away from the more frenetic pace of having to make the proverbial hay while the midsummer sun is shining. The new energy of midsummer can begin to bring a sense of calm returning.

Around the world, midsummer can be a time of expansion and growth throughout all of nature. According to travel-blogger Jurga, who writes under the moniker 'Full Suitcase', June is a perfect time to visit some of the national parks in the USA. Over there, the temperatures are not yet at their peak either, but snow has melted in some of the higher points of Yellowstone. Jurga writes that 'since bison and elk calve in late spring and early summer, there are lots of baby animals on Yellowstone at this time of year', bringing that sense of positivity and possibility. Jurga also notes the opportunities to see bears in Yellowstone at this time, and over on the west coast, it is whale season. Across northern Europe, swathes of land bloom with wild poppies, daisies and buttercups. Meanwhile, in the southern hemisphere in December (their midsummer) bright-red bottlebrushes are in bloom, along with Christmas cactus and waratah – the official emblem of New South Wales.

While our observations of nature are very much tied to the geographic locations that make up our little worlds, I would encourage you to start recording what you see – and let me know. I love hearing how things differ in every corner of our miraculous globe. For the seasoned nature enthusiast, wherever you look at midsummer, wherever you are, the world is full of wonder.

And yet, considering our themes of healing and positivity, we should pay heed to the well-being of our planet and the dramatic consequences of human influence on it. Despite midsummer bringing the natural world to its zenith, the reality is the earth is not full of health and abundance. If we want to manifest health and abundance for ourselves, we must take much more seriously the health of the interconnected ecosystems and webs of life that enable the planetary systems on which we rely for air, water, food and shelter. Ultimately, we will not thrive if they are not thriving too.

TRY THIS: A RITUAL TO CELEBRATE MIDSUMMER

In the week leading up to your midsummer ritual, think about the successes you have had this year, especially those you haven't allowed yourself to celebrate. Often, we move on from our small victories thinking, 'Right, what's next?', without taking a moment to pause and acknowledge them. This is the opportunity to bring *all* your achievements forward and to take the time to give thanks. Spend a few minutes with your journal free-writing all the things that have made you proud during the last few months. It might be as big an event as completing a major piece of work or speaking up for yourself in a tricky situation, or just a small accomplishment, such as making the incense above.

In this ritual, we are going to call on the solar gods associated with the natural world at midsummer – Apollo, Helios, Ra, or any solar being of your choice – for acknowledgement of our successes. If you adhere to another religion, you can call upon the god(s) with which you feel most comfortable; if you are agnostic, you can call on your inner sovereignty.

You will need:

* Your altar, placed in the southern part of the room if possible, and decorated with a yellow or gold cloth
* A yellow or gold scarf
* A yellow candle
* A glass of the dandelion orangeade you made (orange juice is a decent alternative)

If you made a midsummer crown, wear it for this ritual. Begin by lighting your yellow candle. As you do so, recite the following lines:

> Time the devourer will blunt the lion's paw,
> Yet they who stand astride the broad-faced
>   mountain
> Soaring to a peak along the western ridge
> As the great sun rises to its zenith
> Will learn the measure of their success.

Bathed in gold, Mother Nature stands before us,
The corn is still green, the orchards are preparing
    to fruit
And give promise of her harvest yet to come.
The land is heavy with green and the air is laden
    with scent.
Today I stand at the noon of the year
Before swift-footed time moves me ever onwards.
I may wear the crown and not yet feel the gold
So I will pause, and give thanks for my lessons
For without them, who would I be?
For although they may sometimes be born of
    pain
Even amongst the dirt, gold glistens and green
    shoots appear.

Using the notes you made in your journal, say out loud and accept one story of success that you have enjoyed this year. You can list a few more, but after each success you acknowledge, lift your cup and drink to that success.

Next, we are going to take some inspiration from ancient Greece, where it was customary to follow a fourfold process when worshipping a god. Kneel in front of your altar space and follow these steps:

1. Greet your chosen god in as many of their names as you can, especially those relevant for this ritual and time of year.

2. Remind the divine force of all the good things that you have done for him or her in the past year, especially anything you have not yet made time to celebrate. For example, you might choose a deity connected with

nature, and highlight the ways you have been protecting and encouraging nature in your neighbourhood; or perhaps a deity associated with removing obstacles, such as Ganesh, and describe a time you were able to step outside of your comfort zone and achieve something new.

3. Request a favour of the god for the coming twelve months.

4. Thank the god for the help given to you so far and offer a formal act of devotion in their name when the favour has been granted. This does not mean that you'll need to sacrifice a living thing, but that you will dedicate a particular undertaking to them in return. No one else needs to know about it – it is an agreement between you and that divine being. Remember to honour the contract when the time comes.

When you have finished this process, read aloud this invocation to the solar deity taken from the ancient Hymns to Horus, transcribed from the temple walls in Egypt:

> You joyfully stride across the heavens, all your
>   foes cast down.
> The stars which never rest hymn you
> As you sink to rest in the horizon.
> You are beautiful at morning and at evening,
> You speak and the earth is flooded with silence.
> Oh, great hawk whose feathers are many
>   coloured,
> Shining lord of Delphi,
> Wearer of the solar disc,
> Great being who rides the solar chariot across the
>   heavens

From dawn until dusk,
I acknowledge your stillness.
Grant me the ability to see where my strength lies
So that I may have the courage to gaze up into
   your shining face.
Bolts of the doors, thrust yourselves back;
Keys open the doors, for the god is no longer far
   away.
As I leave the safety of my altar
And step back into the world outside
I go with the golden light of hope in my heart
For the harvest yet to come.

In the coming days and weeks, between here and Lammas, it's important to keep reminding yourself of your accomplishments. You might think you don't do nearly enough, but sometimes the detail is in the small things we forget to celebrate. If you feel your sovereignty slipping a little, relight a candle on your altar and sit for a few moments wearing your solar crown (even if it is only in your imagination). Our next turn of the Wheel will be taking us from the zenith to the first harvest, but in the meantime take the time to enjoy and really appreciate how far you have come in so short a period.

CHAPTER SIX

LAMMAS

1 AUGUST (NORTHERN HEMISPHERE)
1 FEBRUARY (SOUTHERN HEMISPHERE)

There were three men came out of the West
Their fortunes for to try
And these three men made a solemn vow
John Barleycorn must die

They've ploughed, they've sown, they've harrowed him in
Threw clods upon his head
And these three men made a solemn vow
John Barleycorn was dead

Robert Burns

THEMES: The first harvest, the cutting of the corn, sacrifice, nourishment, giving
PLANET: Mars
DIRECTION: South-west
TAROT CARD: Strength
ASTROLOGY: Leo

The first of August in the northern hemisphere – and the first of February in the southern – marks Lammas, or the First Harvest. For those who are new to the Wheel of the Year, or perhaps spend little time thinking about the pattern of the agricultural year, this might seem like unfamiliar territory. However, you do not need to travel very far outside of the city to see the cornfields growing golden in the summer sunshine in the lead-up to Lammas.

Lammas marks the first of three harvests that take place over the next three sabbats – the grain harvest (Lammas), the fruit harvest (autumn equinox) and the blood harvest (Samhain). We have already passed the midsummer solstice point, so the days are growing shorter, but we are also still likely to be locked in the intense heat of summer. Meadowlands will be whirring with crickets, and the insect life is vigorously going about its business in the woods and by the waters. Farmers will be harvesting corn, wheat and barley before drying it prior to threshing – to separate the wheat from the chaff.

It might come as a surprise that Lammas is ruled by Mars, the planet and Roman god of war, but in our agricultural past it was common for foot soldiers to come from the farming community. If a war was being fought at the time of Harvest Home, battles had to pause for the warriors to return to bring in the harvest. This was a time for community and fellowship, as the whole population had to pull together to bring in the harvest before the rains came. For, as my diary at Lammas shows, we are already tipping towards autumn.

Lammas weekend – and lavender buds are becoming brown. How quickly everything turns, with whispers of autumn arriving. The first unripe acorns, the first blackberries – tart, but lovely. Wind rustling through oak leaves and the dull hum of city traffic pierced by sirens. I've been exploring new places – stretching out beyond my comfort zone again. There are hawthorn, sloe and elder berries on the trees, though they are still green, and the rosebay willow herb is standing at shoulder height, beautifully in bloom. The smells are intense this weekend and the hardest thing to describe. Savoury, green, vetiver and patchouli, mixed with violet leaf and a top note of jasmine or neroli. If I were soap-making, I would design a whole new blend and call it 'Lammas in the Woods'. On the farm, the oak trees have little patches of bark worn away at their base, which makes them look like elephant feet – the roots are exposed a little way up. Its where the pigs have been pushing their snouts into the earth and rubbing their backs against the trees.

What's happening where you are?

JOHN BARLEYCORN AND NOTIONS OF SACRIFICE

Lammas comes with an edge of sadness to the celebration, with the notion that for every harvest a sacrifice must be given for the gift received. Indeed, one of the themes of Lammas is the idea of 'blood on the corn', referencing the blood red of the poppies that grow among the barley, the blooms that now represent remembrance of our fallen servicemen.

While the grain was growing, it offered refuge to the wildlife thriving within the safety of the corn stalks – field mice and birds nesting, crickets chirring and hares bounding, all invisible in the tall crops. Suddenly, with the tall, graceful stalks cut down, startled creatures are exposed and caught unawares – even trapped by harvesting machines if the field isn't cut outwards. The whirring of the crickets is silenced, and the fields can look bare and stubby.

It was once common to leave one last sheaf of corn standing in the field after harvest, to be cut as part of the sacrificial element of the Lammas celebrations. In traditional folklore, this is the sheaf that represents the spirit of the crop – John Barleycorn.

John Barleycorn is the harvest equivalent of the sacrificial god who is cut down in his prime to sustain us. It is possible that he stems from the Anglo-Saxon mythical figure of Beowa – whose name derives from an Old English word for 'barley' – though in different parts of northern Europe this corn spirit takes different forms.

In Wicca we acknowledge death as part of the natural cycle of life. Life force itself is everlasting in a continuum, but each individual living thing must die or, as the Bengali polymath Rabindranath Tagore beautifully wrote:

> Man is immortal; therefore he must die endlessly.
> For life is a creative idea;
> it can only find itself in changing forms.

We are all subject to the natural cycles of birth and death, and sometimes death brings with it a sustaining force for the living who are left behind. In the case of John Barleycorn, he is sacrificed to make bread and brandy or ale.

If the theme seems familiar to you, the sacrificial god is common in many religions – the sun (or son of) god, who is given to the earth to sustain or save humanity, only to be sacrificed and then rise again to offer renewed hope of the spirit eternal.

The much-recorded folk song that recounts the story of John Barleycorn tells of this sacrifice:

> They've let him stand till midsummer's day
> Till he looked both pale and wan
> And little Sir John's grown a long, long beard
> And so become a man
>
> They've hired men with the scythes so sharp
> To cut him off at the knee
> They've rolled him and tied him by the way
> Serving him most barbarously

The sacrifice of John Barleycorn aside, there is a cost to the bounty of harvest time. Reaping the corn is itself hard work, but there are several more steps to go through before getting to the goodness inside.

Once cut down by the sickle or the scythe, the grain has to be processed, which is another arduous (and allegorical) endeavour. It must be dried and then separated from the stems by threshing or winnowing. Historically, this was done in rural communities by beating the stalks with a flail to separate the grain. The final torturous part of the process was grinding or milling using a millstone – or if you had to do this by hand, a stone quern – to turn the grain into flour.

The toil required at Lammas can be seen as a reflection of the idea that what is life-giving is often also interwoven with pain. While this might sound gloomy, it can help us to make sense of the messy, complicated parts of our lives. After a particularly harsh break-up, I had a sustained period of solitude, which was safe and uncomplicated. Sooner or later though, I had to acknowledge that to find love I needed to open myself to the possibility of further loss. This doesn't mean I am advocating a form of self-flagellation, but opening your heart to love also means opening yourself to the possibility of grief. That threshing of John Barleycorn, then, becomes a metaphor for the process we must go through in life: learning, growing and coming into our power as fully developed adults can be a painful process, though one that can also bring great bounty.

TRY THIS: JOURNALING TO REFRAME YOUR SACRIFICES

As you might imagine from the name, reframing takes a seemingly negative experience and tunes into its positive aspects. I am not going to subject you to the distressing notion that there is always a reason why bad things happen. However, we do sometimes need to rediscover an element of hope and to remember that, as with the harvest, our sacrifices or trials can make us stronger or even become life-enhancing.

For example, when I began my PhD studies around the age of forty, I was desperately seeking a career change. I was applying for jobs all over, but there was one snag I kept hitting. Although I had a master's degree, was enrolled on a PhD programme and my studies were going well, I didn't have the magic formula to land a job in academia – I needed experience of teaching at a university. This infuriated me for a long time. The spells weren't working; the job interviews weren't working. Eventually, I decided that the feelings of frustration were unhelpful, so I set that ambition aside for the time being to concentrate on my community-based teaching (witch classes), charity career and my writing. Later, when circumstances changed and the Covid pandemic threw us all into disarray – and online working – I relocated to my original home on Dartmoor with family close by. Writing in my study several years later, with my puppy sitting by my feet and having just been for a walk and a swim (my idea of heaven), I can see that had I got my wish and landed that job, I wouldn't be here now writing this book.

Using your journal, think about some of the biggest sacrifices you have made in your life. Looking at the bigger picture, let's see if we might be able to 'reframe' them as your gift to your family, your loved ones, to the community or even to yourself.

* What was the nature of the sacrifice?
* What did it mean to you at the time? What did it mean to you one year later? Five years later? Ten years later?
* How does your perspective of that event change when placed within the larger context?

Whatever you think about how your younger self dealt with a particular situation, remember to treat yourself with compassion. Hindsight can be a wonderful thing if you use it to learn from the experience, and not as a scourge to punish yourself.

CELEBRATING LAMMAS

At Lammas, our witches' circle will be embracing the themes of the sabbat, decorating with poppies, sunflowers and corn sheafs. We will toast John Barleycorn with the fruits of his offering – eating bread and drinking brandy – and we might symbolically re-enact his sacrifice.

As a solitary practitioner, there are many ways you can celebrate this festival without a group of people around you.

- Make bread by hand: a great way of getting in touch with what it takes to produce something as basic as bread. See the 'Try This' below.
- Make a corn dolly: there are some lovely (and simple) instructions online, including on the nurturestore.co.uk website, which demonstrates (with pictures) how to make a plaited corn dolly using wheat or raffia.
- Decorate your altar with seasonal produce, including wheat, grass, poppies, sunflowers or whatever grows in your garden or local area and won't deprive pollinators of what they need.
- Meditate on the Wheel of Fortune tarot card and the idea that the Wheel keeps turning and we move from lack to abundance and back again: these symbols can help you delve more deeply into this festival.
- Crown yourself the monarch of your own harvest (why not give yourself a little credit?) and weave a crown out of seasonal foliage as a variation on the midsummer 'Try This' (see page 111).
- Arrange a harvest festival feast for some of your nearest and dearest. It's a good excuse for a dinner party, but if you're not a lover of cooking, make it a bring-and-share event. When you've feasted, try the 'Toast, Boast and Oath' on page 135.
- Research the traditional folk songs that would have accompanied the local harvest festival where you are.

TRY THIS: A RECIPE FOR SIMPLE BREAD

Making bread is one of the traditional ways of celebrating the harvests and the resulting flour of Lammas (which itself derives from an Old English word that translates as 'loaf mass'). As part of my 'year and a day' training prior to joining a coven, I was instructed to make bread by hand to put myself in touch with each stage of the process between field and plate.

You will need:

* A large mixing bowl
* A clean dishcloth
* Some greaseproof paper
* A baking tray
* A damp cloth handy – your hands will get quite sticky
* 500 gm of strong white bread flour – you can substitute this with other flours: I also like to work with spelt, an ancient grain high in fibre that has been cultivated since 5000 BCE.
* 1 teaspoon of salt
* 1 teaspoon of honey or sugar
* 1 sachet of fast-acting dried yeast
* 3 tablespoons of oil – I prefer to use olive, but again you can substitute what you have
* 300 ml of water
* A handful of raspberries or other seasonal berries (optional)

Mix together the dry ingredients (minus berries) in your bowl, ensuring they are evenly distributed. Make a well in the centre of the flour mixture, and add in the oil, and the water. Mix it well with your hands.

At this point you will need to use your discretion a little – if the mixture is very stiff, add a tiny bit of extra water, 1 dessert spoon at a time. If it is too wet, then add a little extra flour, 1 dessert spoon at a time.

You want the texture to hold together so that you can lift

it out of the bowl without wearing too much of it (as I usually do). Leave it in the bowl for ten minutes, and cover with a clean tea towel.

The next stage is where we really get to work: kneading. Place the dough on a flat, clean surface that you have dusted with a little flour, and lightly dust your hands too. Massage the dough with your hands, making sure you knead it for a good ten minutes or so, as this will help activate the ingredients and make them work their magic. You should end up with a supple and pliable dough.

When you have finished kneading, pop it back in the bowl, cover it with the tea towel again, and leave it to rise for about an hour, or until the size of the dough has doubled. Towards the end of the hour, line your baking tray with the baking parchment, and heat your oven to 220°C.

Now it's time to knock back the dough – punch it a little to get the air out – and pull it back into a ball shape. This whole process is great for working out any frustrations. If you want to evoke the image of the blood on the corn, throw in a handful of raspberries, blackberries or elderberries during this phase.

This is the moment to decide what sort of bread you want. You can portion the dough into several pieces and shape them into rolls or separate it into three long sausage shapes that can be plaited together. Or if you prefer the no-frills option, just place a single ball of dough on the baking tray.

If you opt for the rolls, you can brush the top of them with a little milk, or if you opt for the single loaf, dust the top of the dough with some extra flour and cut a criss-cross on the top with a sharp knife. Bake in the hot oven for about 25 or 30 minutes. It is ready when the top is golden brown and the bread sounds hollow if you knock on its bottom.

Let it cool a little before eating: there is nothing better than hand-baked bread fresh from the oven, served with butter, cheese or your favourite topping.

INTERNATIONAL CELEBRATIONS OF THE HARVEST

Wherever farming exists, there are celebrations of the harvest. It is an organic part of living with nature and relying on her for our food, well-being, inspiration and spiritual practices. This means there are myriad harvest festivals across the world, each one focusing on the speciality of the region. However, the timing of those festivals might vary depending on when specific crops are harvested. For example, Thanksgiving, the US festival that marks the first successful wheat harvest of the Pilgrim Fathers in 1621, takes place on the last Thursday of November, while, in Bali, May brings the rice harvest, the goddess of which is honoured with effigies placed in the fields, while festivities are held in the towns.

Slightly closer to Lammas in temporal terms, Iwa Ji (the New Yam Festival) is celebrated in Nigeria at the end of the rainy season (usually between early August and early September) by the Igbo people. Iwa Ji commemorates the abundance of the harvest of yams, which is a crucial crop for the Igbo. The night before Iwa Ji, any old yams must be discarded. The next day, yams are offered to the principal god – the Chukwu – and the ancestors before being distributed among the people. This central ceremony is followed by dancing, masquerades, parades and parties. As the Igbo people have spread across the world, so has Iwa Ji.

Harvests are celebrated by almost every people, reminding us that although many of us live in towns and cities, our rural heart is still beating and is essential, not only for our food sources, but for our spiritual and cultural sustenance as well.

TRY THIS: TOAST, BOAST AND OATH

This is an activity to do in a group with your favourite people – a variation on harvest feasting and the traditional toast. It's something I have done with my coven from time to time and was introduced to me by an Italian *strega* (witch) I know. This 'toast, boast and oath' cuts through the painful English reserve beautifully.

It's a simple premise: each person takes it in turn to toast, raising a glass of your drink of choice to whomever you want: ancestors, gods, living people you have particularly appreciated this Lammas.

The boast is just what it suggests. All share something that you have achieved this year of which you're rightly proud. It doesn't have to be something showy – it can be as modest as you like.

The third part, the oath, is a promise to fulfil going forward, particularly something that pushes you out of your comfort zone. Perhaps it's going out for dinner on your own after a painful break-up, or launching that project you've been mulling over for months, or finally posting pictures of your hidden artworks online.

When all three rounds are complete, we like to have a nourishing meal together and each bring a dish to share with the rest of the group to cement our bond.

A TIME OF NOURISHMENT

The long days of summer are growing shorter as we move back into the dark half of the year, and so in our witches' circle we turn our attention to the coming winter. This might feel early but, as our ancestors knew, the year tends to fly by at an alarming speed. It's important we ensure that we have enough to nourish ourselves and our loved ones, both physically and emotionally, through the long winter months. You never know when you might need a little bit extra to sustain you, whether that's a taste of summer by way of a jar of homemade jam opened on a dull day, or a happy memory, or a realisation that you can come back to in the weeks and months ahead.

In the modern world, this preparation might be more mental than physical, as we can more easily access what we need through the winter. If, however, you are a gardener, there might be things you do in autumn to prepare your garden for the coming frosts of winter: harvesting lavender and turning it into lavender sachets; deadheading flowering shrubs such as roses and hydrangeas, perhaps drying some of the late flowers for use through the winter; or turning your summer fruit harvest into preserves.

You could also see for yourself how the miracle of the harvest is progressing, whether that's marvelling at the rapidly ripening crops in the fields, the blushing tomatoes on your balcony or the wild plants going to seed in the cracks of the pavement, ensuring next year's growth. Cultivating this connection to nature's cycles can be an uplifting experience, allowing harvest time to nourish us both in body and in spirit as we move towards the next turn of the Wheel and beyond. It is also an excellent way of reminding ourselves of the bigger picture: your efforts are never wasted, even if you don't yet feel that your personal harvest – those new projects or fresh perspectives – is quite ready to bring home.

This is only the first of three harvest festivals – we still have the harvests at autumn equinox (fruit) and Samhain (blood) to come. It might be that the nourishment you seek still requires a little more time to grow on the tree, and a little more tending and focused attention before it will ripen.

You might also wish to reflect on how you can share your harvest with others. There is little to celebrate when we consider only our solo position – harvests are better if they can benefit and sustain a circle of people beyond ourselves and be enjoyed together.

In keeping with those ideas, spend some time with your journal free-writing around the following ideas:

- What stores can you put away now to sustain you through the long dark nights ahead?
- What are you harvesting in your life right now?
- What have you poured your loving attention into this year?
- Is it yielding any fruit or are the berries only just beginning to develop?
- What additional nourishment might that crop require in order to carry you through to the harvest?
- How might your harvest benefit others as well as yourself?

TRY THIS: A RITUAL TO CELEBRATE LAMMAS

In preparation for this ritual, think about the areas in your life where you have had to make sacrifices, and the rewards you might have reaped because of this.

If you can lay down any negativity around those sacrifices and what you had to give up, even if you gained something in the process, then I would encourage you to do so. Feel free to include any objects that may represent this sacrifice or harvest and make space for them on your altar.

In addition, you will need:

- An altar set up with tealights or candles (unlit), including a red candle. Place your altar in the south-eastern corner of your room (if you can).
- A plate with fresh bread (whatever kind is the speciality of where you live or just your favourite).

* A bowl or glass with brandy or beer (you can opt for non-alcoholic options if you prefer).
* Corn or barley shoots to decorate, in homage to the grain and fertility gods. Otherwise, in the days leading up to this ritual see what is flowering or ripening where you are, and (ecologically) gather a small amount of seasonal greenery to place on your altar.
* A dish of grain (if you have wheat, fabulous, if not, use whatever is local to you; if you can't source the whole-grain, flour can be a good substitute).

Sitting or kneeling at your altar, tap your glass five times as if beginning a toast, and say the following:

> I stand beneath the stars
> Looking out over my harvest.
> This is the night of the grain,
> The generous king must make his sacrifice,
> The goddess of the land will sustain me.
> In the moment I cut my corn, I birth abundance.
> The gods of the land are present.
> This is the night of birth, and sacrifice, and
>   reward.

Light the candles on your altar, beginning with the tealights, but wait to light the red candle until you say:

> My warrior spirit is coming back to the garden of
>   my self
> On this night I honour my sacrifices and
>   celebrate my first harvest

Lift the dish of grain and run your fingers through it. Feel the texture, and the weight as you say:

> Great god(s) of nature
> I honour your gifts
> Through hunger you sustain us
> Through grief you console us
> Through life you nurture us
> Without honour or reward
> On this night, I remember you

Sit for a moment and gaze at the red candle's flame, and the abundance of nature's gifts on the altar in front of you. Think back over the summer that has passed. What have been the themes for you? On what have you been focusing your energies? Take three deep breaths before you continue.

Move the plate of bread and your glass close to you. Tear off a piece of bread, and name one of your own sacrifices: 'I name the sacrifice of __'. (If you are unsure about your losses and gains, you can refer back to the 'Try This' section on reframing your sacrifices.)

Then eat the piece of bread, lift the glass and toast the harvest it became, saying, 'I honour my harvest of __', as you take a sip.

Repeat this process as many times as you like and, as you do so, envision yourself becoming whole again, drawing back to you all the energy that was lost in the process of the cutting of your corn. Then say:

> As the grain is planted in the earth
> As the sky pours forth sunshine and rain

And the earth yields her own gift of growth
Until the grain is sacrificed again
I take into myself the first harvest
Gaining strength from its rewards
The plate and the bowl are passed forward
Gifts become sacrifices become gifts
In an ever turning spiral of life
Each offering that is lost is gained
And so it is.

Drink from the glass one last time and spend some moments in the presence of yourself and your divine nurturers and give yourself some love and respect for how far you have come. When you are ready to return to the other world, take three deep breaths, and feel the strength and courage returning to you.

I am hoping by this stage you can see the value in these momentary points of pause and reflection. When the pace of modern life can feel overwhelming, connecting back to a more steady, rural-based tradition, adopting a slightly less frenetic pace, even just briefly, can offer a moment of respite and help us thrive within this rapid pace of change.

Our next stop on the Wheel will continue this theme of nourishment and harvest, as we inch towards the next sabbat: autumn equinox.

CHAPTER SEVEN
AUTUMN EQUINOX

21 SEPTEMBER (NORTHERN HEMISPHERE)
21 MARCH (SOUTHERN HEMISPHERE)

Where are the songs of spring? Ay, Where are they?
Think not of them, thou hast thy music too,—
While barred clouds bloom the soft-dying day,
And touch the stubble-plains with rosy hue;
Then in a wailful choir the small gnats mourn
Among the river sallows, borne aloft
Or sinking as the light wind lives or dies;
And full-grown lambs loud bleat from hilly bourn;
Hedge-crickets sing; and now with treble soft
The red-breast whistles from a garden-croft;
And gathering swallows twitter in the skies.

John Keats

THEMES: The wild hunt, the fruit harvest, wisdom and expansion
PLANET: Jupiter
DIRECTION: West
TAROT CARD: The Wheel of Fortune
ASTROLOGY: Libra

At autumn equinox, we have reached our second point of pause in our Wheel of the Year. This equinox, like its vernal counterpart, brings the day and night hours into perfect balance, just as the Libran scales, the astrological sign that rules this time, suggests. However, while the spring equinox was all about the creativity and inspiration of new beginnings, as well as the slight edge of chaos that can come with fresh ideas, the autumn equinox has a more sombre edge.

The folklore of this moment reminds us of the winter that is now galloping towards us, and the themes of this sabbat contain deep contrasts within, mirroring the feeling of being between times. Firstly, we have the second of three harvests – the sweet yielding of fruit that brings a sense of plenty, generosity and expansion – presided over by the planet Jupiter, which rules the autumn equinox. However, the tarot card of the moment is the Wheel of Fortune, the card that reminds us that 'this too shall pass', turning from abundance to absence, success to failure, birth to death, light to dark – and round again. And so it is that during autumn equinox we meet opposition as well as balance; it's perhaps helpful then to look for ways to move more fluidly between the extremes during this period – in the knowledge that the Wheel will turn again.

THE FIRST SIGNS OF AUTUMN

In the northern hemisphere we are watching the leaves begin to turn and fall during this equinox, with all the vibrancy and richness this entails. In early autumn, the sunlight is still softly diffused through the green, though the sycamores and horse chestnuts are already glowing gold and oak leaves are becoming mottled.

Here, in my nature diaries in the run-up to the equinox, we can see this tension between the light and the dark, the end of summer and the push towards winter:

> After a week of intensely humid heat, miserable skin and thunderstorms, we have at last got cold wind, rain and grey skies. I am back in welly boots and waterproofs. Dragon trees are turning to blaze and acorns are falling. It is back to being just me and the crows in the woods and fields. The other birds are silent or absent. We have very suddenly been dropped into the middle of autumn. There is no gradual turn of the seasons this year, it is the flick of a switch. Misty morning, shafts of sunlight and steam rising from the fields with their long shadows. In the woods, a carpet of orange horse-chestnut leaves nestles conker treasures. Cobwebs are spun between every upward-growing spear of grass or plant life.

And a few days later, it is as if summer is making a final valiant attempt to make its mark before retreating:

> Red-beaded berries adorn the hawthorn, the paths already littered with yellow leaves. The grass is losing its emerald flush and has turned dull. And yet this morning has brought with it blue skies, sunshine and warmth again. The sun breaks through a cloud and makes a run for it across the grass. Yet the blackberries are out in force and the wind has a chill edge

144

to it. The quality of light has changed too. It is darker this morning. The streams are running again. Coming to the lake I startled a grey heron, a symbol of water mysteries, of resilience and independence. It takes off, circles three times, and then flies away.

In the orchards, apples, pears, plums and other stone fruits have ripened, and are beginning to fall from the heavy branches. In the woods the trees are laden with sloes, with acorns and with hazels. It is also the time to harvest the last of the berries and nuts; to gather, preserve and store away summer's goodness to feed us through the coming winter, whether as jams and preserves or brewed into a cheeky bottle of sloe gin to add a bit of warmth to cold evenings to come. Of course, today we also have the option of freezing stewed fruits to top steaming porridge or transform into a crumble. Alongside game, this beautiful produce is a part of the celebration of the harvest in the here and now.

LETTING GO

Autumn equinox happens on or around 21 September. The coming of this turn of the Wheel of the Year is always a mixed blessing. It brings with it a profusion of colour and texture, but also a wistful sense of regret for the passing of the summer green for another year. If we must face a certain level of sadness, we do so knowing that the Wheel will keep turning ever onward, and behind the winter will follow another spring, and so the cycle will continue.

There's an internet meme that has been doing the rounds over the last few years that speaks to the idea that in autumn the trees are about to teach us how beautiful it is to let things go. While the authorship of this seems a little hazy, the sentiment is still valid and it is an important point to be considered right now. In witches' circles, we do think about how we can lighten our load before the coming of winter. One suggestion is to take an autumn leaf and write on it what you need to release this sabbat. Head to a windy spot and let the leaf go. As it lifts, visualise that quality, memory or person drifting away from you on the breeze.

To our Druid cousins, who also share the Wheel of the Year practice, this connection to trees is just as important. Not only are they an essential part of our local ecosystem, in our language of nature different trees have come to symbolise different qualities, with signs that can be read in the movement of their leaves. The solid, steady energy of the kingly oaks in the wood, for example, has a very different quality from that of the whispering beeches at home – sometimes seen as the protecting and nourishing mother trees of the forest for her copious offering of nuts to animal and human alike.

In urban centres, trees are especially important. In London, there is a particular species unique to this region: the London plane. This hybrid tree cross-pollinated from the Oriental plane and the American sycamore during the seventeenth century and today makes up much of the canopy of the inner city. This majestic, wide-spreading tree traps air pollution, helping create much needed cleaner air. Toxic particles get stuck to its bark and are trapped in the hairs of its leaves, which the tree then sheds as its bark breaks away in large flakes. This gives their trunks a beautiful mottled appearance in browns and greens.

Trees can also help us to process our own toxins and transmute them into something cleaner and more positive. They can do this physically by way of tinctures, essential oils and teas made of their leaves, but can also help us let go of what's no longer needed – both energetically and emotionally.

TRY THIS: GROUNDING WITH THE HELP OF A TREE

This exercise was taught to me by a dear friend on a day when I was feeling particularly frazzled. It's a great thing to do when you need to pause frantic thoughts or reconnect to your feelings, so that you can start to ground and calmly consider the ritual in letting go that comes at the end of this chapter. This one comes with a warning though. There is a certain amount of 'tree-hugging' involved, and this may look slightly odd to people who don't follow a natural path. But it works, so try to enjoy it!

Find a tree towards which you have a feeling of connection. There is no overt, logical instruction for this; it is all down to your instincts. If this is a new experience for you, relax and try to trust your intuitive response.

Begin by placing your feet firmly on the ground and taking three deep breaths, allowing yourself to 'land' within your body and be present.

Stand facing the trunk of your chosen tree, making sure that your hands, heart and forehead are touching its bark. Visualise all your swirling thoughts draining out of you and into the belly of the tree. Feel the sense of relief as all that unwanted energy passes out of you, as if you have pulled the plug and let all the water out. The tree will take on that energy, neutralise it and push it back out into the soil. It's an exercise in creative imagination and faith.

If your conscious mind is blocking the process and telling you all this is ridiculous, park those thoughts for a moment. Encourage your playful side and do this exercise with a non-chalant air or wait for a moment when you are on your own in a quiet corner of the park. Or, better still, do it with a friend, and then it will just look as though you are having a moment.

Once you feel that your energy is coming down to a more peaceful level, turn and place your back against the trunk, and visualise the tree filling you up with its own energy and strength. As I mentioned previously, different types of trees will have different qualities, and through experimentation you may find that certain species are better suited to different purposes. I like to imagine my backbone getting straighter and stronger as I do this.

Once you feel you are topped up and ready to return to life, leave a small offering for the tree by way of thanks – a hair, an acorn, a drink of water or a small token of gratitude. Please make sure it is something natural and biodegradable. This means no strips of cloth tied onto trees to symbolise wishes or prayers, though I know in some circles they are popular. You might wish to sit under the canopy of the tree for a little while after, enjoying the transitional mood of this season.

A TIME OF TRANSITION AND FLUIDITY

Pagan faiths tend to be polytheist, meaning they recognise many gods, and are fluid about what deities we connect to and work with. In witches' circles, however, our principal deities are the Moon Goddess and the Horned God, with the lighter part of the year presided over by the goddess and the darker part by the god. Autumn equinox signals the moment of transition between the two. While the summer months place an emphasis on the sacred feminine, the winter reminds us to honour the sacred masculine also – not the toxic, patriarchal masculinity that is so damaging to all gender identities, but the healthy version that allows for more balance and is not interested in dominating with outmoded ideas of inequality and control.

When we speak of gender in Wicca, we consider it as a spectrum, not as a binary system that must be only one or the other. Our concepts of masculinity and femininity do not necessarily denote biological gender, but characteristics from the spectrum that runs through all of us, whatever your gender identity. Wicca is essentially a matriarchal religion – our covens are led by a high priestess – but each coven is autonomous, and there is no overall governing structure. Each coven also has a high priest, which reflects our views of deity, and the importance of encompassing all genders.

The notion of an equal separation between dark and light at autumn equinox exists for a split second only, before the pendulum – or the sun at the equator – reaches its zenith and begins to swing the other way. Likewise, we live our lives in the spaces in between, in nuances, and not in the binaries to which some people are determined to reduce everything. Recognising the fluidity in our lives can help us to go with the flow a little more, as when we deal in absolutes we lose the beauty and the subtlety that is already contained in nature.

THE HORNED GOD AND THE WILD HUNT

As the Horned God takes his place with this turn of the Wheel, the story of the hunting of the stag is brought to bear in our witches' circles.

In this allegory, the antlered god calls us into the woods for winter. He tells us: 'Fear not to find me in the darkest recesses of the woods of your soul, for I will always return you to the springtime when our time together is over.' He is both the hunter and the hunted, but he is also the conservator of the forest, and the guardian of the animals. In literature he is the Gentle Huntsman who appears in Sylvia Townsend Warner's *Lolly Willowes*; he is *Lady Chatterley's Lover*, the gamekeeper, Oliver Mellors, who lives in the woods, but is also responsible for managing them. We place his symbols on our altars at this time of year: the black candle and horns, seeds and berries from the trees outside.

It's worth noting here that when I use the word 'horn' or 'horned', I am referring to stag horns or antlers. Despite what you might have heard, Wiccans don't worship the devil. To begin with, the devil is a concept that comes from organised religions – Satan in Christianity, for example, and Shaitan in Islam. There are theories that these iterations of the devil are based on a demonised version of the Greek god Pan, who has goat feet and horns, as well as a voracious sexual appetite.

Archaeology has discovered evidence of the antlered figure that predates organised religion by a long shot. In France, there are Palaeolithic cave paintings that show antlered male figures and in Star Carr in Yorkshire twenty-one horned ceremonial head-dresses were uncovered that are thought to be about 11,000 years old. Individual antlers have also been uncovered at Stonehenge, Brean Down and Wasperton, while coins found in Cirencester and Petersfield show an antlered figure thought to date back to the year 20 CE.

One of the best (and most well-known) examples of an antlered figure is the one on the Gundestrup Cauldron, an artefact made almost entirely of silver, uncovered by peat cutters in Denmark. It is thought to date to 300–200 BCE. The Gundestrup figure sits cross-legged, with a torc in one hand (signalling rulership) and a serpent-like figure in the other. He is surrounded by creatures, including a deer, potentially signalling his position as 'Lord of the Animals'.

While archaeology gifts us with an array of antlered artefacts, the stag appears as an important theme in folklore too. In Welsh mythology, while the king is out hunting the stag, he encounters his underworld counterpart, hunting the same quarry. In this instance, the stag becomes a crossing-over point, as the two kings trade places for a year and a day. In Berkshire, there are the varying legends of Herne the Hunter. Some tell of Herne being out in Windsor Great Park when an arrow is fired at the king. In one version Herne steps in and takes the fatal shot, while in other versions he is shamed for committing an act of treason and in his despair hangs himself from an oak tree in the forest. In all instances, he then returns in death as the protector and conservator of the forest, a figure akin to that on the Gundestrup cauldron.

In Jacob Grimm's version of the Herne legend, Herne is placed in the role of the leader of the wild hunt, a pack of ferocious riders who are seen mainly at night. Folklore contains a plethora of these wild hunt stories. It's a trope that is found across Europe, from the Norse god Odin, leading the hunt across the skies, to Dewar and the Wisht Hounds swirling out of the mists on Dartmoor, where it is whispered he is the devil. All these tales have one theme in common: the hunting of men's souls, and the inevitable coming of disaster or death. If you are caught out alone when the great hunt rides, then you will perish, unless – in the case of Odin – you carry iron, salt or parsley to protect you.

Folklore can fill the gaps in the record that archaeology cannot, and all these tales have become part of the crucible that is the autumn equinox.

WATCHFULNESS AND THE LANGUAGE OF THE NATURAL WORLD

While there might not have been any stags to see in North London in autumn (and they are just as rare where I live now), there was a herd of stallions I liked to have close while writing. They would often be in full gallop around their field, having just rounded the top of the hill in front of me, tossing their heads, bucking their hind legs, and snorting at each other. Their dramatic display sometimes forced me to pause and watch in wonder, a colder bite in the air as I sat beneath the turning leaves of an oak.

Following the Wheel of the Year can facilitate a deep level of watchfulness. Life forces are communicating with us all the time if we are willing to pause, watch and listen from within. Mary Webb described this as hearing with the soul, and not the ears. The horses' dramatic display felt as if it had been put on in my honour, and I was replete with awe and gratitude at being able to witness it. It felt like a message, a sign that I was on the right track and sufficiently plugged in to the natural world to hear those messages.

Energetically, my consciousness rode with them for a time. However, watching them also helped me to take in more of my wider environment, the horses alerting me to the approach of other human beings making their way up the hill. The herd was unsettled for a time, until the source of the loud noise came into view – a group of young children with their mothers, searching for conkers. The horses then settled back into grazing, cropping the grass short and swishing their tails to send the late flies packing.

A single white stallion continued his interest, coming up to the fence to see what I was doing on the bench, what was keeping me so absorbed. No one who comes face to face with so beautiful and noble an animal can ever doubt its intelligence. Continuing to insist that humans are superior to animals is sheer folly and arrogance in my book. All creatures are sentient beings deserving of respect.

The sudden appearance of animals can be read as a form of communication, depending on what that creature symbolises. When I was spending too much time procrastinating and not enough time writing, the universe used to send me countless spiders. They invaded my tiny flat and would spin their webs wherever I looked. Every time I sat down in a park or outside, I would find at least one or two crawling over me, much to the hilarity of my closest friend, who had to keep removing them. The spider symbolises creativity, and it was as if nature was literally instructing me to start spinning my web of words.

Often, the signals start quietly, but if you continue to ignore them, they get louder and larger until you pay attention. As soon as I started significant work on the novel, the spiders went away. Likewise, a quick search for the meaning and symbolism of horses told me what I already knew in my unconscious, that horses symbolise masculine energy, inner force and a passionate nature. All those qualities we celebrate in the god at the time of the autumn equinox.

WALKING ALONE IN AUTUMN

Astrologically, autumn equinox is ruled by the sign of Libra, the scales, which is characterised by balance, tranquillity, acceptance, fairness and diplomacy. It is a good symbol to hold in mind as we continue our search for ourselves in this particular sabbat, and do so on foot. It is often in the quiet moments of movement that we rediscover ourselves, and realise we were there all along.

Autumn has always been one of my favourite seasons for watching the minutiae of the changes flowing through the natural world. As temperatures start to drop and daylight hours wane, walking can also make this a more comfortable experience, keeping up our body temperature.

Growing up in a national park, I was spoiled by miles and miles of open moorland through which to walk. Close to the city, some footpaths can feel a bit of a tease, giving you a glimpse of untamed nature before abruptly and unexpectedly depositing you back into the urban landscape. There is so much open space that is fenced off and to which we don't have free access, and – like the Right to

Roam campaigners – I would love to see this access extended and the countryside opened up for us all to expand our wisdom of ourselves and the world we share.

Wherever you live, the challenge is finding what's most comfortable and available to you. Paul, who is a photographer on Dartmoor, recently joined me for a walk there. While some folk often refer to this land as lonely or bleak at this time of year, Paul told me about how some of his photography students begin to find themselves in these quieter places. 'It's fascinating how quickly people get it, when I tell them I am just going to photograph a tree over the top of the ridge and let them get on with it for a short period,' he tells me. 'I leave them slightly nervous but come back to find they have really understood the gift of solitude, having entered it knowing it's only for a short time.' With daylight decreasing and the weather getting colder, autumn can make it easier to find these moments of solitude, a time to rebalance, but not everyone is able to bear being alone.

In my twenties, I took a group of Londoners to Dartmoor to shoot some scenes for a feature-length film we were making. The group consisted of some very burly chaps who were playing the parts of gangsters and drug runners, but they were afraid of the autumnal darkness, and the apparent loneliness of the spot. They felt unsafe and anxious with so few people around in the miles and miles of deep, seemingly unending, night. Having grown up in this solitude, I feel the opposite – much safer in the loneliness of a rural area than the dark of a city.

In modern life, we are simply not used to darkness or being alone, and yet, if you go to places that offer this, you are more likely to have space to connect to your inner self in a way you simply can't among the bustle. Try this in a way that feels safe to you. On an autumnal evening walk, it can still be warm enough to carry the whirring of the crickets, and a song thrush busy singing from a

nearby elm tree, long into the evening. It is only when we are prepared to face the darkest skies that we begin to see the stars.

TRY THIS: GETTING TO KNOW YOUR LOCAL FLORA AND FAUNA

During my pre-initiation coven training, one of the tasks set
for me was to map out my local area and its wildlife. This
meant that if I was asked to gather a bough of yew for a
Samhain ritual or some oak leaves for midsummer, I would
know where to find them. It also meant I was able to put
down firmer roots in an area that didn't always feel like mine.
I now tend to do this in any new area to which I move as a
way of helping me to settle.

For obvious reasons, it is easier to do this in the verdant
months, identifying plants and trees when they are still holding onto their leaves or blooms. Yet in autumn, their changing
colours and textures can tell us just as much about their char-
acter and personality, with sculptural seed pods that can be
just as effective for discovering species that are new to you.

Why not try this in your local area? Either find or draw a
map of your immediate vicinity – it can be as small as your
garden or as big as your town. Then mark on it the natural
landmarks you have already encountered on your sojourns
in nature. Which trees stood out for you? What flowers were
in bloom? Which birds nest where? Do you know the location of a hedgehog hideout or host of sparrows? Is there a
pond rich in insect and aquatic life? The more you immerse
yourself in a particular area, the more you can add to your
map, increasing the layers of meaning and memory until you
have created a rich tapestry of the flora and fauna that make
up your home ground.

IDENTIFYING YOUR HARVEST

As winter comes towards us, gathering us into its long nights and short days, our attention will turn inward. This is the beginning of a time for introspection.

When we are working with the unconscious, the mythology of the Wheel and the big themes of life reflected in the natural world, the layers we peel back go deeper every time. As the years pass and each sabbat comes round, I learn something new about it and about myself. After twenty years of practice, I am indeed intending to die a beginner.

By following the Wheel and engaging in an almost constant cycle of expansion and wisdom-gathering, we learn more about ourselves and our place in the world, thereby creating an increasing sense of balance and trust. When we can recognise our personal cycles and preoccupations, we often cease to be quite so afraid of these when they begin. An old friend of mine used to refer to this as a 'life laundry'. By following a theme around each sabbat, we are sorting through our piles and making each one a little more manageable to process. Each year you might find that the same sabbat has a slightly different nuance as you start to work through them again, each time learning a new layer of meaning.

In your journal, have a bit of free-writing time framed around the following questions for this sabbat:

- What have you harvested this year?
- Will it be enough to see you through the winter?
- How much do you want things to remain static, how much to change?
- Where have you achieved a feeling of balance in your life?
- How might you work with the sense of life always flowing onwards?

Here are some more ideas for how you might celebrate autumn equinox and mark a shift in perspective.

- Visit a local orchard (if you have one) to spend some time with the apple trees and harvest a few apples – with permission.
- Gratitude lists are a great way to celebrate another kind of harvest. In your journal or notebook, list seven things you are grateful for.
- Balance can often come by taking care of your physical surroundings and having a bit of a declutter can help send out the 'stuck' energy and restore some balance. Perhaps it's time to 'autumn clean' your living space in time for winter.
- Apple crafts: make cider, apple chutney, apple jelly or, even better, apple and blackberry crumble.
- Create an autumn feast with seasonal berries, nuts, vegetables and, if you eat meat, game of some kind. Sharing apple cake, cider, brandy and apple juice with friends, for example, is a wonderful way to celebrate the offerings of a single fruit.
- Build an autumn equinox altar and spend time at it reading seasonal poems. You might start with John Keats, who stands at the head of this chapter.
- Get out and walk in the woods, and make sure you swish your feet through some autumn leaves (yes, it's compulsory!).

TRY THIS: A RITUAL TO CELEBRATE AUTUMN EQUINOX

In the run-up to this ritual, have a think about the themes we explored in this chapter and in its exercises. When and where do you need stillness in your life? Where would you like more movement inwards or expansion outwards? How might you embrace a sense of fluidity and ease at autumn equinox? As winter approaches, are you ready to travel into darkness – the place of your fears but also your dreams?

For this ritual, you will need:

* A black candle
* Your altar, placed in the west and decorated with a black altar cloth (if possible)
* An apple (you can substitute any autumn fruit from where you are for this, but it works best if it's a fruit that is firm with edible peel)
* A cocktail stick or a toothpick
* As many candles as you like to place around the space
* Some seasonal greenery to decorate the room and your altar
* A handful of autumn leaves
* A marker pen – this doesn't have to be a permanent pen. We are going to write on the leaves, and it doesn't matter if the words are illegible – you will know they are there.
* A glass of apple juice or cider

Prepare your room in the usual way – clearing and cleansing both you and the space.

Decorate your altar in whatever way is pleasing to you, with the altar cloth in place, the black candle at the centre and the seasonal greenery and leaves. I quite like placing a vase of seasonal plants behind the candle (not so close that they might catch fire). If you can, place your altar in the western point of the room – the compass point for this sabbat.

Begin the ritual by grounding yourself with three deep breaths. Light the tealights or candles in the room, and then return to your altar. If you're able, sit cross-legged like the Gundestrup antlered god. Then say:

> Once more a moment of pause in the dance
> As autumn sweeps in with the cold wind.
> In front of me the scales of balance;
> Behind me the summer sun.
> Which way will I go?
> Westward, towards the setting sun.

Hold the autumn leaves in your hand and continue:

> The trees in their finest raiment
> Remind me of all I must let go
> And among the branches, jewels.
> In this moment, my pledge.

Light the black candle and meditate on the flame for a few minutes. Think of all the things that no longer serve you, the things you must let go in order to move forwards. Don't worry if this feels daunting – it is natural to cling unconsciously to some of our old, ingrained patterns, and can be intimidating to step outside them. Think instead that you are freeing yourself.

Take up the pen, and on each leaf write down the name of the thing you are letting go. Then say:

> I call upon my guides and gods to bear witness
> And so steady my resolve.
> I pledge this to myself:
> I love you;
> I believe in you;
> I will nurture you.

At this point, if you can, open a window and fling those leaves out for the wind to carry them away. If you do not have access to an open window, crush the leaves up in your hand, saying, 'I release you – I release you – I release you', as you do so. If you need to stamp on them a bit too, go ahead. At the end of the ritual, make sure you sweep up all the debris and leave none behind. If you are doing this outdoors, I find that taking the leaves to a high place is a good alternative. However, make sure you do it as you must let go of that energy in some way. Don't keep it hanging around.

Once done, take three deep breaths. Do you feel any different? Just notice, don't judge.

Raise the glass of juice or cider and say:

> The sweetness of self-belief
> I may hold in escrow
> In trust of that harvest
> This my pledge

Drink from the glass and know that you are on your way.

Pause for a moment at the altar and focus on the qualities you'd like to replace those old ones. Put them into single words.

Take up the apple and the toothpick and write the words on the apple. As you do so, really focus on how you will feel when you have those qualities. What will the world look like, smell like, taste like, sound like and feel like when you are there?

When you have written all you want to on the apple – you can write as many things as you can fit on it – then really look at it. See the progress happening, and say:

The sweetness of self-belief is upon me
Each step forward
Tips the scales in my favour
I call in that which is mine
As the hunter marks the prey
I chase down my dreams
Through the woodland glade of night

Then eat the apple and, as you do so, visualise taking those qualities into yourself with the nutrients from the fruit.

When you have finished, end with a simple:

And so it is.

Record in your journal any thoughts or impressions you wish to take away with you. This means you can chart your progress over the coming weeks and see what develops.

Don't worry if things take time to filter through – very often with magical and internal work the results can be subtle, but trust that things are changing.

As you move from late summer into early autumn and beyond, consider how far you have come, and who has helped you along the way. We have spent some time exploring the concept of solitude and expansion in autumn equinox, but no person exists alone in the world. As the Wheel of the Year turns towards the next sabbat – Samhain – it will encourage us to connect to the important task of remembering those who went before us.

CHAPTER EIGHT

NOVEMBER EVE OR SAMHAIN

31 OCTOBER (NORTHERN HEMISPHERE)
1 MAY (SOUTHERN HEMISPHERE)

How can you lie so still? All day I watch
And never a blade of all the green sod moves
To show where restlessly you toss and turn,
And fling a desperate arm or draw up knees
Stiffened and aching from their long disuse;
I watch all night and not one ghost comes forth
To take its freedom of the midnight hour.
Oh, have you no rebellion in your bones?
The very worms must scorn you where you lie,
A pallid mouldering acquiescent folk,
Meek habitants of unresented graves.

Adelaide Crapsey

THEMES: Honouring our ancestors, death
PLANET: Saturn
DIRECTION: North-west
TAROT CARD: Death
ASTROLOGY: Scorpio

The end of October brings with it Samhain (pronounced SOW-en, SAH-wen or SOW-ain). After Beltane, this is probably the most widely known Wheel of the Year sabbat. It is also my favourite stopping point on the Wheel of the Year – not the commercialised version of Halloween with plastic pumpkins and nylon witches' hats, but the thoughtful, reflective version.

Samhain is one of the festivals that is truly old – dating back two thousand years to the dark ages. In Irish mythology, this was the time of year when secret doors could be opened between the worlds of men and the fae. In other parts of the British Isles, stories emerged of people being pixie-led on this day – folk who went into the mist and returned seventy years later, unaged and unchanged. This was the night when the worlds of the living and the dead were deemed closest and the souls of the departed were said to return for one night only.

The themes of this festival, then, speak to how we view death and how we honour our ancestors, whether familial or otherwise. This focus at Samhain is no bed of roses; there are no unicorns – but in my own practice I find this far more resonant and uplifting than any number of 'bright blessings' you might care to wish me, for there is much to learn.

However, before we dive into this chapter, it's worth noting that the use of language around this festival can sometimes be problematic (although arguably not as problematic as Mabon and

Lughnasadh, which were arbitrarily added later). Some pagans suggest that unless you are of Celtic origin, the use of the word 'Samhain' could be construed as cultural appropriation. Language can be a dividing force in many situations and, while it might not be an easy thing to reconcile, awareness is key.

I am going to use Samhain and November Eve interchangeably in this chapter, as that is what my tradition taught me, and as my paternal ancestors came south from Leith, I feel comfortable in this.

FACING OUR MORTALITY

We are now firmly in the dark part of the Wheel of the Year, presided over by the male deity who is the god of death and resurrection: he meets us at the gates between the living and the dead. Our poetic and sacred writings for November Eve really home in on that point, and speak of the gentle embrace of death that awaits us all.

Themes of death and resurrection are common in old myths and legends as people come to terms with the inevitable onset of winter before new life emerges in spring. In ancient Egypt, we have the story of the goddess Isis and her consort, Osiris, who is murdered by his brother, Set, in a jealous rage. Osiris is transformed into the god of the underworld and recognised as the god of death and resurrection – his green skin representing his ability to bring fertility to the land. Meanwhile, in the Greek world view, we encounter the story of Demeter and Persephone. While out in the meadows painting the flowers, Persephone is abducted by Hades, Osiris' Greek counterpart, and taken to the underworld. This sends Demeter, her mother and the goddess of nature, into deep mourning. Through a twist of the story, Demeter is able to rescue her beloved daughter, but because Persephone was tricked into eating six pomegranate seeds while in Hades, she must return there for half the year, thereby throwing the world into winter as Demeter mourns afresh.

This sabbat was once a time when people would inevitably have to face their own mortality, as not everyone in the community would make it through the coming winter alive. While – some might say – we have grown used to creating an unhealthy distance from thoughts such as these, the presence of death is still always all around us as it is a natural part of life. If you have experienced the loss of a loved one, or if you have worked in a setting where loss of life is common-place (such as healthcare), you will understand this. Coming face to face with death is a necessary and transformative experience in life, and one that will change you forever.

This is also the time of the blood harvest. As we've seen, trad-itionally there were always three harvests in preparation for winter: the grain harvest we saw in Lammas, the fruit harvest at autumn equinox; and now the blood harvest, when livestock would have been slaughtered. While the blood harvest might sound like some-thing you would encounter in a horror film, it stems from a practical and logical approach for rural communities to take when facing the prospect of the cold season. The meat would be salted down to preserve it through the winter, to provide much needed food but also so that poorer owners did not have to feed and shelter the animals through the spartan season. Samhain would, therefore, be the last point of the year where you could eat fresh meat.

A popular phrase at Samhain describes it as the time 'when the veils are thin', a night during which the souls who have left the physical world can return and wander the earth, where they can see and be seen. You might find lots of online references to this speaking with apparent authority about it being an ancient Celtic tradition. While I really love the image this conjures up, I am afraid this is another of those scenarios when I am about to place a spanner carefully in the works. Although the concept of the dead visiting us is an ancient one, the idea of 'veils' is probably another modern invention.

Adrian Bott, who writes about the historical origins of pagan ideas and rituals, suggests that there are no pre-Victorian references to the veils being thin at Samhain: rather, it is an idea that was born of the world view of the Spiritualist movement. The earliest reference he has detected comes from Ralph Whitlock's *In Search of Lost Gods: A Guide to British Folklore*, published in 1979. Bott argues that the ancient Celts would not have seen a distinction between the worlds of the living and spirits, as the divinities did not so much exist on planes as in physical places. This makes the idea of there being veils between them nonsensical. As Bott writes:

> The less magical the world was believed to be, the more it became necessary to posit a division between us and the realms of wonder . . . In summary, Samhain is not a time when the Veil grows thin, because there never was a Veil in the old tales, and magic was *everywhere*.

As Bott goes on to say, this is not a criticism of such ideas. If you are particularly attached to a bit of lore, if you are aware of its probable origins, it doesn't have to stop you enjoying it.

DARKNESS AND STILLNESS

Samhain marks the point where we enter the dark part of the year. In the UK, our clocks have been put back an hour, the nights are drawing in, and the dawn comes a little later still each day. Nature is turning inwards – the world has turned amber, and the first storms of winter are upon us. In the hedgerows are a good haul of sloes, rowan, hawthorn berries and rosehips, which, according to plant lore, should be gathered following the first frost. The cold winds will be blowing through the branches while, in the undergrowth, small animals rustle in the leaf litter. The trees have mostly shed their leaves and are also turning their energy inwards in order to survive the harsh winter that lies ahead. Yet they do so in anticipation that the Wheel of the Year will keep turning, that spring will eventually follow the darkest night and that their leaves will return. Already, if you look carefully on many trees, you will see the tightly furled buds of next year's leaves, just waiting.

There is a stillness and an internal focus that has started to take root and that will see us through winter. Rather than feel frustration at how this interferes with the usually fast pace of life, try to let go of any expectations and breathe in the stillness. Stillness brings tranquillity, which brings insight. Insight brings understanding, and understanding brings wisdom, with a renewed sense of purpose.

This is the crux of being a follower of a natural path: when we live a more watchful existence, sometimes we need a little patience for the insight to come. There is rarely any rush, but we convince ourselves that we must get there quickly (wherever 'there' is).

In the days running up to Samhain, I would encourage you to slow down, breathe, open your eyes and look with wonder at the beauty of the autumn leaves on the trees that line our streets, and the fine details of their branches that are revealed as the leaves fall. Pause and listen for the chattering of the few remaining birds, such as robins, just audible over the noise of the traffic. Stop on the street and look at the clouds passing overhead, or the fungi growing on the sides of trees, and don't worry if you are met with the odd tut from passers-by. The chances are they have forgotten the beauty that surrounds us.

TRY THIS: A RECIPE FOR ROSEHIP GIN
This is a favourite of mine, but if you can't find rosehips (the seed pods of the dog rose or *Rosa canina*) and you do

have sloes, then go for it – I rarely follow an exact recipe and am always substituting ingredients with what's to hand. Similarly, this will work just as well with vodka as it does with gin.

Take yourself out to the hedgerows and see what you can find. The last remaining berries are an important food source for birds, so, whatever you take, please replace three-fold with an alternative – if you gather one cup of rosehips, leave behind three cups of bird seed.

You will need:

* Approximately 500 g of ripe rosehips (or sloes or damsons, etc.)
* 250 g of sugar
* 1 litre of gin (or vodka)
* A 2-litre bottle or glass jar, or two 1-litre jars

When you have gathered your hips and fed the birds, wash the ripe pods carefully, and pop them in the freezer overnight to help the skins split. You can also do this by poking them with a cocktail stick or giving them a quick bash in a pestle and mortar.

The next day, put the frozen rosehips in a bottle or glass jar and add the sugar. Pour the gin over, give it a good shake so the sugar starts to dissolve, and then store the mixture in a cool, dark place. Give it a good shake once a day for the first week, and then leave it to 'cure' for two to three months. I find if I make this at Samhain, it's ready in time for midwinter.

When the gin has fully cured, then you can strain out the pods and rebottle (if you want to). I often leave it as it is as I like to see the hips or berries.

MOURNING THE LOSS OF A LOVED ONE

My own relationship with Samhain relates most directly to its connection with grief and mourning. When I was younger, my mother died very suddenly due to a very aggressive form of cancer, a loss that was catastrophic. I hate it when we talk of death in terms of 'loss' as it suggests you have just been rather forgetful, so my choice of language is usually direct on this subject. However, when she passed away, I spent most of the first year in a state of amnesia, forgetting most of what was going on around me, and frequently disabled by great heaving bouts of weeping. I experienced what I can only describe as a hollowing-out of the self. When my mother died, so did my own identity. I could no longer remember what I liked to wear or eat, or even what I liked doing. I forgot everything except her.

Turning to my own path for answers gave me scant relief. At that time there were very few pagan works on grief and loss. This meant that trying to make sense of what was happening to me within the context of my own spirituality was very hard, and it had to be done through my own personal gnosis – the knowledge that comes from lived experience. The public side of pagan life frequently focuses on the happier aspects of living, but when you have midwifed your own mother's passing and come so closely face to face with death that you can feel its breath on your cheek, no amount of herb sachets or crystals will put you back together. I tried to write, but the words had ceased flowing; I tried to paint, but all I could do was smear large amounts of black paint across the canvas. My teacher has always told me that the language of ritual is poetry, so it was there that I turned for solace.

In my weeks and months and years of grief, it was the nature writers (who I refer to as my Nature Mystics) who consoled me. Mary Webb suffered a comparable paroxysm of grief when her father died when she was in her thirties. D. H. Lawrence had a similar response when his mother passed away, and he produced some of the most gut-wrenching (but soul-relieving) grief poetry on the planet. One of my favourite poems, which I turn to at Samhain, is Lawrence's 'The Ship of Death'. In it, he explores the inevitable death and rebirth of the self that comes with grieving.

> Now it is autumn and the falling fruit
> and the long journey towards oblivion.
> The apples falling like great drops of dew
> to bruise themselves an exit from themselves.
> And it is time to go, to bid farewell
> to one's own self, and find an exit
> from the fallen self.
> Have you built your ship of death, O have you? . . .
> Build then the ship of death, for you must take
> the longest journey, to oblivion.
> And die the death, the long and painful death
> that lies between the old self and the new.

When grief comes to call, it changes us irrevocably, and in a way that is unequivocal. It makes us realise that the control we thought we had over our lives and our loved ones is ephemeral at best, illusory at worst. But there is a quote that springs to mind at this time of year, although I have been unable to attribute it (answers on a postcard please if you know it!): 'In autumn the trees are about to show us how beautiful it is to let the dead things go.'

HONOURING THE DEAD

Samhain gave me my focal point, a stopping place in which I could pause and reconnect with my mother, and let her go in faith that one day we might be reunited. I began to make and burn incenses to her, out in the open air, willing the smoke to deliver my message of love, wherever she was now. Finally, I started to write again. Samhain is the time we remember those who are gone, knowing that we will come back to their memory with another full turn of the Wheel of the Year.

In witches' circles at this time, we bring in images or remembrances of our loved ones, and our rituals are given in honour of our ancestors. In fact, I will go one step further and say that while we often invite our honoured dead into our circles at any time of year, at November Eve we wouldn't dream of holding a rite without them.

Looking across the world, this is one of those 'collective unconscious' moments, as many cultures hold festivals and rituals in autumn, all with a common theme: reverence of our ancestors and a remembrance of our dead.

Anecdotally, I was once told by a resident of Upper Egypt that in his home community near Luxor, at this time of year families visit the cemetery and take a meal to eat with their ancestors. Even as far back as the Roman Empire, there are reports of a festival called Feralia that celebrated the *lemures*, the spirits of the restless dead who would need to be appeased to prevent them from making mischief, and although it did not fall into the same period of the year, it is likely that this would have merged with Celtic and Druid practices as the Roman Empire spread. In Romany cultures, families have an active approach to remembrance, with visits to the cemetery including the loved one's favourite drink being libated on the grave.

In Mexico there is Día de los Muertos, or the Day of the Dead, which is very much a day of joyful celebrating, as opposed to deep mourning and grief (the further I travel away from my own bereavements, the more I appreciate this celebratory aspect). The blessed ancestors are celebrated with *calaveras* – representations of the human skull, which provide a much needed reminder of our own death-to-come – and the bright-yellow Aztec marigold flowers. Altars are dressed at home, and *ofrendas* are placed on them, usually the favourite food and drink of the departed. It is here that the tradition of the 'dumb supper' originates, a time when the family gathers to eat, and lays an extra place for the spirit of the loved one who has passed. In recent years, there are now also parades, with people going out into the streets dressed as skeletons. All these ceremonies are ways of reconnecting with those who have gone before us and bringing their presence back into our lives, while recognising our own mortality.

Christian faiths celebrate All Hallows' Eve or All Saints' Day on 1 November in honour of the Christian martyrs. All Hallows is thought to date back to at least the year 800, when churches in Ireland and Northumbria were marking the day. Others claim Frankish origins to the festival, although records are hazy.

Historically, across the British Isles, this was an important time of celebration even before the arrival of Christianity, the last big festival before the coming of the hard winter ahead. In Scotland, however, Protestantism wiped out many of the traditional folk celebrations at this time of year.

Yet where small pockets of Catholicism remained in the Highlands, some traditions were protected. These included the four points of the year when homes were purified and the fires were put out, and then relit afresh – the cross-quarter days, which included Samhain. Farmers would lay bonfires in fields to cleanse them, and the traditional foods at this time included apples, nuts, parsnips and carved turnips placed in windows either to scare the spirits away or to welcome them in. In Ireland people would dress up as the spirits and go out among the houses. There was also a Scottish tradition of creating two large bonfires which folk walked between to 'cleanse' themselves. In England, these cleansing fires survived but were merged with the Guy Fawkes celebrations of 5 November, which took over from many of the elements of the traditional holiday festivities, according to Ronald Hutton.

It's worth discussing the elephant in the chapter at this point, one I've mentioned only briefly so far – Halloween. While Halloween has its roots in Samhain, the name itself comes from the Christian festival of All Hallows' Eve.

With the British colonial rule of Ireland and the devastating potato famine in 1845, large numbers of Irish people were forced to emigrate and the festival travelled with the diaspora to America. Pumpkin carving evolved out of a practical necessity: the traditional turnips were unavailable in the New World and so were replaced with this easily accessible squash, which were probably much easier to carve than a tough old turnip in any case.

Just as with Christmas and Santa Claus, the American version of Halloween has become a melting pot of different cultural traditions from across the world. In recent years, mostly thanks to its portrayals in popular culture and increasing commercialisation, what many of us know of Halloween has come back over the Atlantic from the United States in a beautifully meandering motion.

In my grandmother high priestess's coven, November Eve was sometimes referred to as 'Hallowe'en', and that was certainly the festival I grew up with as a child in my little rural community on the moors. We would go to gatherings in the village hall where apple-bobbing and fancy dress were part of the festivities. Trick-or-treating is more popular these days, although it didn't feature in my childhood, partly, I suspect, because of the geography as much as anything else. (One year some friends and I decided to go carolling at Christmas, but with several miles between the houses, we did more walking than singing.)

But while Halloween is undoubtedly a fun festival to celebrate, it has become a commercial holiday that is largely related to fancy-dress parties and trick-or-treating, and it is a very different thing to Samhain. Samhain retains its roots as a spiritual festival, one that is reverent and respectful of the souls of the departed.

CONNECTING TO OUR ANCESTORS

As well as offering an opportunity to pause, and connect to my mother and other family members who have passed on, for me Samhain provides a space to focus on a wider sense of ancestral connection too.

Whenever life calls us to rebuild ourselves from the foundations up, ancestors can be crucial in that process. Whether you believe that the spirits of those ancestors are actually helping you, which is closer to the Wiccan view, though each Wiccan will have their own take on this, or whether those ancestors become your inspiration or road map for a journey, it doesn't much matter.

If you find a void when you look to your biological ancestors – perhaps you have been cut off from your family or exiled from your land – then I would invite you to turn instead to what Armistead Maupin, the author of the wonderful *Tales of the City* books, calls the 'logical family'. An 'ancestor' can include those who have walked your path before you in numerous different ways.

For instance, I have my spiritual ancestors, the ones from my tradition and my line in Wicca, such as the community leaders of the past, writers and practitioners alike. In my first year of grieving, I was studying tarot with Tomas d'Aradia at the amazing Treadwell's bookshop in London. It became a weekly joke that every time one of my classmates tried to read for me, up popped the Death card, toothily grinning and waving from astride his horse. The card itself relates to endings, but also the transformation that can occur when we embrace those endings and allow them to occur without resistance. Endings also become beginnings. It is sometimes interpreted as 'death and a new beginning' or 'transition'. The Death card followed me closely for several years and, over time, I learned the lesson of this tarot card until I could give an in-depth analysis of its every angle.

The Death card is similar in some ways to the Six of Swords, which represents another transition, showing a journey across water, reminiscent of the 'ship of death' in Lawrence's poem. It was also the card that marked my initiation into Wicca – not all endings and transitions are literal deaths.

Then there are my logical ancestral nature lovers: Mary Webb, D. H. Lawrence and other writers who work with nature as their principal inspiration (and put in an appearance on my altar at this time). Both Webb and Lawrence suffered from serious health concerns (Webb from Graves' disease, Lawrence from tuberculosis) and spent long periods outdoors as a result, focusing on quiet time in nature. Lawrence is quoted as once saying:

> I lose myself among the trees. I am so glad to be with them
> in their silent, intent passion, and their great lust. They feed
> my soul.

You might say that the enforced stillness that came with a debilitating illness probably contributed to the microscopic intensity with which Webb and Lawrence both observed and recorded the minutiae of nature. As a nature writer, I can't imagine two better literary ancestors to consult with on matters of nature observation than them.

The discovery of consoling words from those who have gone before us can bring a sense of kinship on an otherwise solitary path. At this time of year, my little flat in London could feel quite crowded with the presence of all these ancestral spirits, both familial and spiritual. As the Wheel of the Year turned round to

Samhain during that first year without my mother, I finally found some comfort.

While the pressures of modern life can take us away from our land and our familial ancestors, searching and connecting to the geographic ancestors of where you live now can be an integral part of taking root in the place you find yourself in today. While I would not encourage wholesale cultural appropriation, and one should always be respectful and considerate of those whose culture you are exploring, researching local customs and traditions – and then making an appropriate offering to the genus loci – can be an integral part of learning to feel at home wherever you are in the world.

When I moved to London, I struggled with life in the city until I decided to go in search of nature in my local neighbourhood. Eventually, I found woods in the green belt that I could walk in; they gave me solace and made me feel more at home. One day, I was catching up with my dad and telling him about this place.

'What's the name of the wood?' he asked. When I told him, he responded in a very understated way: 'I used to play there as a child with [his brother] John.'

This blew my mind. I knew that Umpa's family had come from Scotland down to London where he met Nan, and that during the Second World War they were bombed out of the East End and displaced. At that point Nan – alone, because Umpa was away fighting – moved her sons to a house just up the road from where I was living. You could put this down to coincidence, but this link to the past helped me to feel so much more connected in the present and to this place. This is why ancestor veneration, whether logical or biological, can form an important part of spiritual practice, whatever denomination you find yourself in.

TRY THIS: A MOMENT WITH YOUR LOGICAL ANCESTORS

If the idea of ancestor veneration is new to you, spend a little time with your notebook or journal thinking about the people you have admired the most in your working life, in your spiritual life, or any other area of your life that brings you joy.

* Who has inspired you the most?
* If you were to hold a fantasy dinner party, and you could invite any six people from history – living or dead – who would you ask?

Those are the people you might choose to focus on at this sabbat.

FINDING NATURE IN QUIET PLACES

In the city, spaces where one can enjoy some peace are often few and far between. Parks are the obvious choice but they can get quite overcrowded. An often overlooked quiet spot to explore at this (or indeed at any) time of year is your local cemetery. I haven't found a church or graveyard yet that wasn't quiet and peaceful, except for the sound of a blackbird singing, or the clack of a magpie or two. In fact, it is often a good spot for connecting with the birds.

As with many aspects of nature, there is a mostly forgotten language of birds and what they symbolise. The divine can and will communicate with you in a variety of different ways, and there is a hidden language in which birds appear to you at different times. For instance, crows and other corvids are a symbol of magic, while owls can symbolise wisdom, or learning. Doves are traditionally associated with peace, while pigeons can represent homecoming.

The lexis of nature is not all that hard to read, just as symbols of dreams are a lot more straightforward than some might have you believe. You can seek out books to decode these for you, or you can trust your unconscious mind to reveal their meanings through meditation, or straightforward questioning. I always prefer to allow my inner self or unconscious mind to do the work, as what one thing means to me may be very different from what it means to you. Following the path of nature is (for me) all about developing a relationship with the divine power all around us.

One of the ways you can utilise this idea of a sentient, ineffable universe is to ask for help with a problem with which you're struggling. I like to take the problem and either 'walk it out' or sit with it in nature to see what insights come. If you allow your internal dialogue free rein in a quiet space, you will much more easily reach a place of stillness within that allows you to listen to what your inner self wants to say. Walking is particularly effective for this as it has a natural rhythm that can act as a form of hypnosis on your conscious brain and calm your 'monkey mind' thoughts. Our unconscious self always has the answers we need; we just have to be quiet enough to hear it.

TRY THIS: VISITING A BURIAL GROUND

Soon after my mother had passed, I used to regret that I couldn't visit the graves of my ancestors as often as I would have liked – they were so far away from where I was. So I developed ways in which I could pay my respects regardless. One was to buy flowers for my mother, but gift them to a friend or family member, or even place them on my altar with a photograph of my mum. Another was to pay my respects by visiting a burial ground near me and gifting the flowers to one of the graves that clearly didn't receive many visitors.

As my mother pointed out before she died, a grave is really a focal point for those left behind. While the loved one's mortal remains might lie there, I don't for one minute think that is where I would find Mum. If I know my mum, she is much more likely to be off having adventures where the fun stuff is happening, or checking in on me or my siblings when we're feeling inspired, down or confused. She won't be rattling around in a graveyard on top of a windy Dartmoor hill.

Exploring the graves in a nearby cemetery can also offer insights into those who surround you in life, giving you a sense of their myriad attitudes and end-of-life rituals. Some might differ greatly from your own. For instance, in Dartmoor my community always marks graves with local granite, and visits there are often a rather sedate affair, whereas my local community in the city favoured black shining marble grave markers and photographs of the departed person, giving a sense of who the person was. There were also a diverse mixture of cultures there – some graves were Jewish, some Muslim, others Chinese and some Polish.

OTHER WAYS TO CELEBRATE SAMHAIN

- Samhain marks an important transition further into the dark part of the year. We stepped over the threshold at Lammas, but at this sabbat we are really committing to this journey. As we've explored, Samhain is a great moment to focus on your ancestors and to invite them in to work with you. One way to do this in your practice is to set up an altar and light candles to them, looking at their picture as you do so.
- You can also hold your own family dinner at Samhain, setting an extra place and inviting your ancestors to join you in the meal. Talk about them and share memories with the other guests. Remember, your ancestors don't necessarily have to be familial; this can be a time when you connect with your 'logical' family

as well as your biological one. Your ancestors might be amazing people that have gone ahead of you in your field of work, historical figures to whom you feel a deep connection, as well as your parents, grandparents and other blood relatives. You will always have ancestors to work with.

- If you have space to do this safely, light a bonfire in your garden. Fire pits are a good way of doing this as they contain the heat and the damage. Do watch out for creatures such as hedgehogs who might be hibernating under any leaves.

- Samhain also lends itself to divination, so now might be the time to try some scrying or practice with that oracle deck you have been eyeing on the bookcase. I find it's important to 'bond' with a deck before you start using it. Making a bag to keep it in and sleeping with it under your pillow for a few nights are good ways to kick-start this process.

- The archetypes of this festival are the gods of death and the underworld, and while the deities are sometimes alarming in their appearance, they can also be very charismatic. There is something strangely magnetic about the concept of journeying to the underworld. Why not gather some friends and experiment with storytelling? One of my favourite methods is asking each person to contribute one sentence to a story about a visit to the underworld. The results are sometimes bizarre, sometimes funny, but always imaginative.

TRY THIS: A RITUAL TO CELEBRATE SAMHAIN

In the week leading up to your Samhain ritual, it is customary to spend some time in quiet contemplation of your ancestors, and how they have contributed to your life. In the days leading up to a Samhain circle, I might place photos of my ancestors on the altar and keep a candle burning for them when I am present. You might also like to think about the legacy you are leaving. How will you be remembered by the loved ones you leave behind?

You will need:

* A bell, or something that will sound like a bell when you strike it. Witches often use bells in rituals as a marker, but also as an energy cleanser.
* A black candle
* Your altar, placed in the north-western part of the room, and decorated with a black altar cloth
* Extra candles or tealights to softly light the room
* Blue fabrics or scarfs to represent the sea or the River Styx that lies between the land of the living and the underworld
* A tarot or oracle deck
* Pictures or mementoes of your ancestors
* A coin for the boatman of the River Styx
* A glass of your favourite tipple
* Your notebook and a pen (optional)

Light the tealights or candles but not the black candle for now. If you can, place your altar in the north-western corner of your room. Lay the black cloth on your altar, and place the black candle in the centre. Then place the photos or mementoes of your ancestors in the opposite corner of the room and place the blue cloths – representing the water – between the altar and your ancestors.

If you'd like to, you can light some incense. There are some lovely Samhain or Saturn incenses available.

Start the ritual by taking three deep breaths and then striking the bell three times. As the sound of the bells fades into the shadows of the room, say:

> The bell rings in the sunset
> As we gather in the harvest of blood.
> For now it is autumn, and the falling fruit,
> and the long journey towards oblivion.
> And it is time to go, to bid farewell
> to one's own self and find an exit
> from the fallen self.
> To stand at the gates of winter
> And face the darkest shadow
> And begin the longest journey.

Start to spiral out from the altar towards the ancestor mementoes. If you want to play music at this point, feel free, something with a slow drum heartbeat would be appropriate.

As you move, do so slowly, and focus on the feeling of your physical body. Does it feel heavy? Light? Are there aches? Don't judge it, just notice how your physical self feels. Sway gently as you move, and gradually come to a stop by the edge of the 'water'.

When you reach its edge, you must be ready with a coin for the ferryman who will carry you across – this is the Six of Swords, the journey across the water (reminiscent of ancient Greek mythology and the journey the dead made across the River Styx to reunite with their loved ones). However, we are making this journey only temporarily, and will return. At the edge of the water, say:

> All that live must die.
> Passing through nature to eternity
> These are but wild and whirling words.
> A dream itself is but a shadow,
> The rest is darkness.

But out of the silence my voice carries:
I call upon the ferryman to aid me in my quest
To cross the waters to the unknown shore
Across the soundless boundless bitter sea.
Bring me now my ship of death
Mine is the way into darkness.

Place the coin in the waters, and step across the divide. As you reach the corner where your ancestor mementoes are, say:

Into the cave's mouth
This darkening night
I peer into blackness
And call you forth.
I open the gates that you may return
For this night only.

Gather up your ancestors and begin to carry them back to the altar. Place them on the altar and light the black candle. As you do so, say: 'May I light the way for you, as you once did for me.' Kneel at the altar and focus on each ancestor in turn. Name them one by one, and out loud state the gift they gave you. Tell them why it was so important to you. Raise a glass and drink a toast to them. There is a saying that people die only when you forget them. By naming them and their accomplishments, we are keeping their names alive.

At this point, it is customary to do a little divination. Don't worry if you don't own a tarot or oracle deck, just meditate on the candle flame instead. As with the scrying we did at Imbolc, it is normal to receive only fleeting thoughts and glimpses.

Kneel or sit at the altar in front of your ancestors and pick up the oracle or tarot deck. If you have incense burning, pass the deck through the incense to bless and cleanse it. Take some deep breaths as you do so. Begin to shuffle the cards and think about your question or what you need guidance on. As you shuffle, say:

> Thank you, ancestors and guides, for telling me what I need to know. I am thankful that you continue to guide me even through the distance that lies between us.

Pull three cards – one for the situation, one for the advice you need and one for the possible outcome if you follow the advice. Lay them on the altar in front of you and meditate on what they represent for a few minutes. Take your time doing this – there is no rush. Once you have finished contemplating the cards, you might choose to write down your thoughts in your notebook. Then, when you are ready to come back, strike the bell three times, and say:

> Once more I stand witness
> As the great Wheel turns
> From birth to death to birth again.
> One day the gates will open for me
> As they did for my ancestors before.
> But tonight, my dear ones can revisit
> And make merry with me in this place.
> Now I must return to my own adventures
> My time to go home has not yet come.

Strike the bell three times to end the ritual. Then make sure you eat something to ground yourself, and stay hydrated.

If you have been with me since Yule, you will now have completed a full cycle of the Wheel of the Year, and its turning has brought us back to the 'beginning' again. You can now choose to leave your observances there, or to continue your journey. What will you deepen your understanding of in your second pass, or your third? Doubtless, there will be fresh discoveries waiting for you at each cycle, as well as new experiences. If you choose to go on, I have no doubt you will find it a rich and fulfilling practice. I did.

DESIDERATUM,
OR THE MANIFESTO OF
PERFECTLY IMPERFECT

*The power of this life, if men will open their hearts to it, will
heal them, will create them anew, physically and spiritually.
Here is the gospel of earth, ringing with hope, like May
mornings with bird-song, fresh and healthy as fields of young
grain. But those who would be healed must absorb it not only
into their bodies in daily food and warmth but into their minds,
because its spiritual power is more intense . . . We need no
great gifts – the most ignorant of us can draw deep breaths of
inspiration from the soil. The way is through love of beauty
and reality, and through absorbed preoccupation with those
signs of divinity that are like faint, miraculous footprints across
the world. We need no passports in the freemasonry of earth
as we do in the company of men; the only indispensable gifts
are a humble mind and a receptive heart . . . No accident of
environment or circumstance need cut us off from Nature.*

Mary Webb

Trying to conclude a book about a process that is a spiral, and not a linear stroll through time, seems somehow incongruous. Yet I have found myself ending, as I began, with the words of my logical ancestor, Mary Webb. Her 1917 book of nature essays, *The Spring of Joy*, proposed that humans must, for their own well-being and that of the planet, return to nature. While we might conclude that life was simpler in the early twentieth century and so this was perhaps an easier proposition, I am not sure that is the case. We might have greater knowledge of environmental issues than our ancestors a century ago, but I believe that like Webb's generation we too have lost our connection to the sacred in nature, and have consequently lost some of our magical sparkle. As Webb went on to say:

> One violet is as sweet as an acre of them. And it often happens
> – as if by a kindly law of compensation – that those who have
> only one violet find the way through its narrow, purple gate
> into the land of God, while many who walk over dewy carpets
> of them do not so much as know that there is a land or a way.

If I have one wish for you in reading this book, it is this. That you may rediscover the sacred nature of yourself and recognise something of the divine – whatever that means to you – in a single flower. I believe, if you have got this far, you already understand that our little spherical part of the universe is a beautiful and special thing, but sometimes we forget that we are part of that sanctity, which can result in environmental destruction and loss of life at all levels. Individually we may be perfectly imperfect, but it is important that we all focus our efforts on preserving this beautiful world we live in.

From twenty-plus years of following the Wheel of the Year, I have found that each time I journey around the sun that the layers of meaning have only become deeper and more nuanced.

One of my favourite ways of working with this spiritual life is to dedicate a portion of it to a particular purpose. If your first turn around the Wheel with me is devoted to nurturing and healing your soul a little, you can then turn subsequent spirals to other intents – perhaps one year can be dedicated to environmental work, another to learning more about our non-human animal companions, another to a great ambition, another to deepening your connection to whichever deity you live with – the list goes on. Or perhaps you might consider spending one turn of the Wheel changing the voice of your inner self to one that is kinder to you. As Tagore taught, life is indeed a creative idea. The great irony this brings is that just as we think we're getting a handle on it, life can pull the joker card on us and surprise us with a new twist. But by following the Wheel of the Year more closely, we can learn to recognise the patterns that emerge in our lives and start to see more clearly how we can manage the surprises as they occur.

Instead of attempting to conclude something that is in fact only partway through, I will instead raise a glass to your continuing fascination with the natural world. Long may it continue.

ACKNOWLEDGEMENTS

Some of you might be expecting a tale of magic to explain how this book came about and, indeed, here it is. I had long thought I would like to write a book on the Wheel of the Year but was looking for the right home for it. So I dutifully placed a sticky note on my 'books I would like to write' wall planner (yes, I have one) and left that seed to rest in the dark while I got on with other projects. In my world, this is referred to as 'surrendering to the gods' or 'leaving it to the Cosmic Joker to sort out', which they certainly did. A short time later, I was chatting with Bernadette Russell, one of those bright souls who does amazing work in the world, lifting other people so they can fly. Bernadette, who was once an attendee at my Wheel of the Year classes but has long since transitioned into a friend, casually mentioned to me one day that she knew someone who was looking for an author to write a book on the Wheel: if I was interested, perhaps she could put us in touch.

No book is ever really the work of one writer in isolation, and this is no exception. It has taken an extraordinary team of people to bring this book to life, to nurture it, and shape it to the point where it can step out into the world. This book has had the privilege of the best possible start. It was birthed through the vision of those early conversations with Sarah Rigby at Elliott & Thompson, whose vision matched my own in every detail, and who manages that delicate balance of allowing the writer freedom to be creative while asking the right questions at the right time to tease out the detail. Also on the team are the fabulous Pippa Crane, who beautifully handled the task of keeping me on track with my research; Jill Burrows, who kept an eye on those pesky words that can sometimes move around when you are not looking; and Amy Greaves, who has worked tirelessly to help the rest of the world hear about it. I feel as if I have found my dream team.

A further tale of magic comes in the form of my agent, who must also make it onto this list. Another task added to that wall planner was 'find a lovely agent to work with'. The Cosmic Joker delivered there too, sending me Michael Alcock at Johnson & Alcock, who manages to bring much-needed encouragement at the right moments. Michael, I think in fact you might be the top banana.

Of course, there are many other people who have helped in countless ways, with kindnesses both big and small. When my own engagement with the Wheel of the Year began over two decades ago, my teacher Christina gave me terrific insights and opened the pathway ahead. To Will, who has organised and facilitated so many of the classes that I have run since, I owe a professional and personal debt of gratitude. The attendees at those workshops asked questions that encouraged me to think beyond the obvious and into more nuanced layers of meaning, as have the magical group of people who have shared my personal practice over the years. Each turn of the Wheel in their presence has yielded more and more harvests and encouraged deeper magical thinking. Then there is my lovely sister, Kath, who on our morning walks allowed my steady stream of consciousness about the book to flow, and Lizzie, who is always a fabulous sounding board. A thank you too to John, for arriving at the eleventh hour to restore my faith in new beginnings (and more of that anon). Each person has their part to play. I am grateful to have had them all in my life.

I can only imagine what the Cosmic Joker will bring in next. I look forward to finding out.

REFERENCES

Introduction

Julia Cameron, *The Artist's Way* (Pan Books, 1995)

Scott Cunningham, *Wicca: A Guide for the Solitary Practitioner* (Llewellyn, 2000)

Ben Aaronovitch, *Foxglove Summer* (Gollancz, 2015)

1 Midwinter or Yule

Mary Webb, 'The Joy of Form', in *The Spring of Joy* (Jonathan Cape, 1928)

'Don't equate your self-worth . . .' Wayne Dyer [@DrWayneWDyer], 24 September 2013, Twitter. Quotation often attributed to Kurt Vonnegut, although no source seems to be given. Perhaps this is one of the great mysteries of the internet . . .

For practising kindness at midwinter: Crisis at Christmas, www.crisis.org.uk/crisis-at-christmas, accessed 15 April 2022

Rabindranath Tagore, 'In Praise of Trees', in *Selected Poems* (Penguin Classics, 2005)

2 Imbolc or Candlemas

D. H. Lawrence, 'Craving for Spring', in *Unrhyming Poems* (Martin Secker, 1929)

For Nana Nicoline Jensen's walks in Denmark, www.moonchildyoga wear.com/blogs/news/silent-walks-and-meditations-how-to-get-a-great-amount-of-energy-by-walking-absolutely-silent, accessed 5 April 2022

3 Spring Equinox

The Trial of Isobel Gowdie, 1662, translated and published in Robert Pitcairn, *Ancient Criminal Trials in Scotland* (1833)

4 May Eve or Beltane

Folk song, 'Padstow May Day Night Song', as published on https://www.cornwalls.co.uk/padstow/obby_oss_may_song.htm, accessed 10 August 2022

Doreen Valiente, *The Charge of the Goddess* (The Doreen Valiente Foundation and the Centre for Pagan Studies, 2014)

Ronald Hutton, *The Stations of the Sun: A History of the Ritual Year in Britain* (Oxford University Press, 1996)

Mary Webb, 'Vie Medicatrix Naturae' (1911), *The Spring of Joy* (Jonathan Cape, 1928)

Sharon Blackie, 'Marrying the land: how we broke the ancient bargain', https://sharonblackie.substack.com/p/marrying-the-land-how-we-broke-the-ancient-bargain, accessed 7 May 2022

Beltane Fire Festival website, https://Beltane.org/about-beltane, accessed 10 March 2022

'Gay Green Gown', https://mainlynorfolk.info/folk/songs/gaygreen gown.html, accessed 10 March 2022

5 Midsummer or Summer Solstice

Folk song, words by Rudyard Kipling, originally published as 'A Tree Song' in *Puck of Pook's Hill* (Penguin Popular Classics, 1995), later set to music and popularised by Peter Bellamy

www.visitgloucester.co.uk/things-to-do/history-and-heritage/cheese-rolling-in-gloucester, accessed 5 June 2022

For Jurga's observations about the American national parks, https://fullsuitcase.com/national-parks-june, accessed 25 April 2022

6 Lammas

Robert Burns, 'John Barleycorn', *The Complete Poems and Songs of Robert Burns* (CreateSpace, 2017)

For instructions for making a corn dolly, https://nurturestore.co.uk/how-to-make-a-corn-dolly-craft-for-a-harvest-celebration, accessed 8 May 2022

7 Autumn Equinox
John Keats, 'To Autumn', *Selected Poems and Letters of Keats* (Heinemann, 1966)
For the British Museum exhibition 'The World of Stonehenge', www.britishmuseum.org/exhibitions/world-stonehenge, accessed 18 May 2022

8 November Eve or Samhain
Adelaide Crapsey. 'To the Dead in the Graveyard Underneath My Window', 1914
D. H. Lawrence, 'Fantasia of the Unconscious' (1922), www.gutenberg.org/ebooks/20654, accessed 2 May 2022
For Adrian Bott on 'the veil being thin' being a modern invention, https://twitter.com/cavalorn/status/924967445303123968?lang=en-GB, which also gives links to his blog, accessed 2 May 2022

Desideratum, or the Manifesto of Perfectly Imperfect
Mary Webb, 'Vis Medicatrix Naturae', op. cit.

FURTHER READING

If something in this book has piqued your interest and you would like to find out more, I would encourage you to track down these titles in your local library or independent bookshop. I keep a regularly updated reading list on my website, so you can always drop by at www.rebeccabeattie.co.uk and find the latest version.

History of Witchcraft and Folklore

Callow, John, *Embracing the Darkness: A Cultural History of Witchcraft* (London: I. B. Tauris & Co., 2018)

Callow, John, *The Last Witches of England: A Tragedy of Sorcery and Superstition* (London: Bloomsbury, 2022)

Davies, Owen, *Popular Magic: Cunning-folk in English History* (London: Hambledon and London, 2003)

Gibson, Marion, *Witchcraft: The Basics* (London: Routledge, 2018)

Hutton, Ronald, *Stations of the Sun: The History of the Ritual Year in Britain* (Oxford: Oxford University Press, 2001)

Hutton, Ronald, *The Triumph of the Moon: A History of Modern Pagan Witchcraft* (Oxford: Oxford University Press, 2019)

Scarre, Geoffrey, and Callow, John, *Witchcraft and Magic in Sixteenth- and Seventeenth-Century Europe* (Basingstoke: Palgrave Macmillan, 2001)

Practical Magic

Beth, Rae, *Hedge Witch: A Guide to Solitary Witchcraft* (London: Robert Hale, 2001)

Cunningham, Scott, *Earth Power: Techniques of Natural Magic* (Woodbury, MN: Llewellyn, 2002)

Cunningham, Scott, *The Complete Book of Incense, Oils, and Brews* (Woodbury, MN: Llewellyn, 2002)

D'Este, Sorita and Rankine, David, *Practical Planetary Magick: Working the Magick of the Classical Planets in the Western Esoteric Tradition* (Glastonbury: Avalonia, 2007)

Wicca

Adler, Margot, *Drawing Down the Moon* (London: Penguin, 2001)

Crowley, Vivianne, *Wicca* (Rockport, MA: Element, 2011)

Cunningham, Scott, *Wicca: A Guide for the Solitary Practitioner* (Woodbury, MN: Llewellyn, 2002)

Curott, Phyllis, *Book of Shadows* (London: Piatkus, 1999)

Curott, Phyllis, *Witch Crafting* (New York: Broadway Books, 2001)

Gardner, Gerald, *Witchcraft Today* (Newburyport, MA: Book Tree, 2022)

Gardner, Gerald, *The Meaning of Witchcraft* (Newburyport, MA: Weiser, 2004)

Green, Marian, *A Witch Alone* (Newburyport, MA: Hampton Roads, 2009)

Mooney, Thorn, *Traditional Wicca: A Seeker's Guide* (Woodbury, MN: Llewellyn, 2018)

Starhawk, *The Spiral Dance: A Rebirth of the Ancient Religion of the Great Goddess* (San Francisco: Harper, 1999)

Valiente, Doreen, *The Charge of the Goddess* (Sussex: Centre for Pagan Studies Ltd, 2014)

The Old Ways

Cornelius, Henry, *Three Books of Occult Philosophy* (Woodbury, MN: Llewellyn, 2018)

Anon, *The Lesser Key of Solomon* (Bristol: Mockingbird Press, 2016)

Culpeper, Nicholas, *Culpeper's Complete Herbal* (New York: Sterling, 2019)

Dunn, Patrick (trans.) *The Orphic Hymns* (Woodbury, MN: Llewellyn, 2018)

Spencer, Craig, *Aradia: A Modern Guide to Charles Godfrey Leland's Gospel of the Witches* (Woodbury, MN: Llewellyn, 2020)

Psychology and Neuro-linguistic Programming (NLP)

Bandler, Richard and Grinder, John, *The Structure of Magic: A Book About Language and Therapy* (Palo Alto, CA: Science & Behaviour Books, 1989)

Jung, Carl, *The Archetypes and The Collective Unconscious* (London: Routledge, 1991).

Poetry and Literature

Beattie, Rebecca, *Nature Mystics: The Literary Gateway to Modern Paganism* (Winchester: Moon Books, 2015)

Williams, Jean and Cox, Zachary *The Gods Within: The Pagan Pathfinders Book of God and Goddess Evocations* (London: Moondust Books, 2008)

Astrology and Tarot

Hundley, Jessica, Fiebig, Johannes, and Kroll, Marcella, *Tarot: The Library of Esoterica* (Cologne: Taschen, 2021)

Pollack, Rachel, *Seventy-Eight Degrees of Wisdom: A Book of Tarot* (London: Thorsons, 1998)

Richards, Andrea, Miller, Susan, and Hundley, Jessica, *Astrology: The Library of Esoterica* (Cologne: Taschen, 2021)